110857973

12 OCT 2009

ESSENTIAL
CANADA EAST

 Best places to see 34–55

Québec 111–148

 Featured sight

Atlantic Provinces 83–110

Ontario 149–186

Original text by Fiona Malins
Updated by Penny Phenix

© AA Media Limited 2009
First published 2007
Revised 2009

Series Editor Lucy Arthy
Series Designer Sharon Rudd
Cartographic Editor Anna Thompson

ISBN: 978-0-7495-6122-2

Published by AA Publishing, a trading name of AA Media Limited whose registered office is Fanum House, Basing View, Basingstoke, Hampshire RG21 4EA. Registered number 06112600.

AA Media Limited retains the copyright in the original edition © 2005 and in all subsequent editions, reprints and amendments

A CIP catalogue record for this book is available from the British Library

Colour separation: MRM Graphics Ltd
Printed and bound in Italy by Printer Trento S.r.l.

A03804
Maps in this title produced from map data © Tele Atlas N.V. 2005  Tele Atlas

About this book

Symbols are used to denote the following categories:

- map reference to maps on cover
- address or location
- telephone number
- opening times
- admission charge
- restaurant or café on premises or nearby
- nearest underground train station
- nearest bus/tram route
- nearest overground train station
- nearest ferry stop
- nearest airport
- other practical information
- tourist information office
- ► indicates the page where you will find a fuller description

Maps

All map references are to the maps on the covers. For example, Ottawa has the reference ➕ 9D – indicating the grid square in which it is to be found.

Admission prices

Inexpensive (under Can$6)
Moderate (Can$6–$12)
Expensive (over Can$12)

Hotel prices

Per room per night:
$ budget (under Can$75)
$$ moderate (Can$75–$150)
$$$ expensive to luxury (over Can$150)

Restaurant prices

Price for a three-course meal per person without drinks:
$ budget (under Can$25)
$$ moderate (Can$25–$40)
$$$ expensive (over Can$40)

This book is divided into five sections.

The essence of Eastern Canada pages 6–19
Introduction; Features; Food and drink; Short break including the 10 Essentials

Planning pages 20–33
Before you go; Getting there; Getting around; Being there

Best places to see pages 34–55
The unmissable highlights of any visit to Eastern Canada

Best things to do pages 56–79
Good places to have lunch; train and boat trips; stunning views and more

Exploring pages 80–186
The best places to visit in Eastern Canada, organized by area

▲▲▲ to ▲▲▲▲▲ denotes AAA rating

Contents

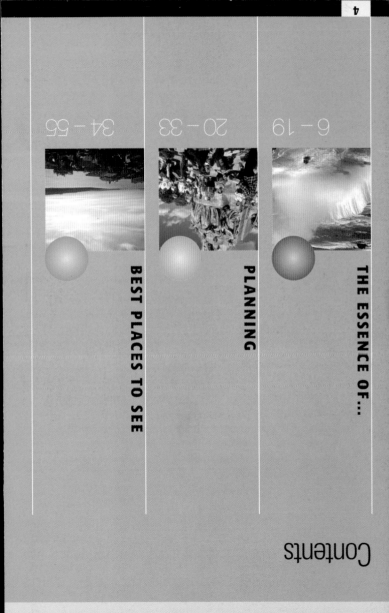

BEST THINGS TO DO

56 – 79

EXPLORING...

80 – 186

The essence of...

Eastern Canada is huge, so don't try to see it all in one go. Instead, include a little of everything during your trip. The Atlantic coast is an essential destination, from the intriguing lifestyle of Newfoundland to the wonderful scenery of Cape Breton and glorious New Brunswick beaches. Inland are more natural beauties: the vast Great Lakes and the popular Niagara Falls.

Eastern Canada also has sophisticated cities. Toronto has fine modern architecture, Montréal abounds in splendid restaurants, Ottawa offers great museums and Québec has a stunning site and a resolutely French face. In all, there's something here for everyone.

features

Eastern Canada is a land of great variety. Nowhere is this more true than in the Atlantic provinces, where you can experience the Bay of Fundy and its dramatic tides, the wild Atlantic coast of Nova Scotia, spectacular Cape Breton, the tranquil beauty of Prince Edward Island and the rugged landscapes of Newfoundland.

The natural beauty of Eastern Canada is complemented by vibrant cities and towns, among them Montréal and Toronto, each one unique in character and charm.

Finally, despite the crowds, don't miss standing on the brink of Niagara Falls watching all that water endlessly falling over the rock edge.

GEOGRAPHY

● Most of Ontario, Québec and Labrador are part of the Canadian Shield, rich in minerals, covered with forest and traversed by fast-flowing rivers.

● The five Great Lakes cover 244,000sq km (more than 94,000sq miles). The deepest is Lake Superior, with a maximum depth of 406m (1,332ft).

● The St. Lawrence River is Eastern Canada's major waterway. Although it is only 1,223km (760 miles) long, its drainage basin covers nearly 518,000sq km (200,000sq miles).

- The highest peak of Eastern Canada is Mount Caubuick (1,652m/5,420ft) in the Torngat Mountains of Labrador.
- Newfoundland and Labrador's craggy coastline stretches for around 9,900km (6,152 miles).

ANIMAL LIFE

- The forests are the domain of many animals including moose, deer, beaver and a variety of bears. The north also has caribou.
- Canada geese are all over the region. They are particularly prominent during migration, when they fly in vast V-shaped formations.
- Several types of whales can be seen around the coast of Nova Scotia and New Brunswick's Bay of Fundy, and in the St. Lawrence near the mouth of the Saguenay every summer (➤ 54–55).

SPORTS AND LEISURE

- Hockey is the national obsession, and it's played on ice of course!
- The fabulous natural countryside of Eastern Canada is ideal for outdoor activities such as camping, canoeing, hiking and fishing, and skiing, skating and snowmobiling in winter.

food & drink

ATLANTIC PROVINCES

Not surprisingly for a region so closely connected with the sea, there is seafood galore here: large, luscious Malpeque oysters from Prince Edward Island (PEI); tender Digby scallops from Nova Scotia; and fat red lobsters from New Brunswick (Shediac is "the lobster capital of the world") and also from PEI, where attendance at a community lobster supper is *de rigueur*. In New Brunswick, the Atlantic salmon is wonderful; Oven Head, near St. Andrews-by-the-Sea, is a great place to buy it smoked.

In Newfoundland, fish and *brewis* (salt codfish and seabiscuit) is a favorite dish, while for dessert you could try figgy duff, a steaming-hot raisin pudding. In the Acadian areas, chicken *fricot* (hearty

chicken soup) will warm you up, or try *poutine
rappé* (potato dumpling with salt pork).

In Halifax, Alexander Keith's India pale ale is
distinctly hoppy in flavor. Drink it with Solomon
Grundy (marinated herring – a touch salty), or
swig it down with
fiddleheads, the tender
curled ends of ferns,
lightly boiled and
slathered in butter. For
a sweet treat, buy
chocolates from
Chocolatier Ganong in
St. Stephen, New
Brunswick, widely
available in stores.

QUÉBEC

There is a small wine industry in
southern Québec and a plethora
of microbreweries making beers
with such colorful names as
Maudite (Damned), Fin du

Monde (End of the World) and Eau Bénite (Holy
Water). As an aperitif or after-dinner drink, try
Sortilège, made from maple syrup and Canadian
whisky, or Chicoutai, made from cloudberries.

The local camembert and brie cheeses are
delicious, especially when eaten with some of the
wonderful breads produced by such companies as
Montréal's Première Moisson. In Montréal, juicy
slices of smoked meat piled high on rye bread is a
tradition brought by Jewish settlers from Eastern
Europe. Alternatively, try some *tourtière* (minced
meat and potato), and finish with *tarte au sucre*
(sugar pie) or *pouding chomeur* with maple sauce.

Apples grown in the Rougemont area are used to
make alcoholic ciders, apple vinegars and even iced

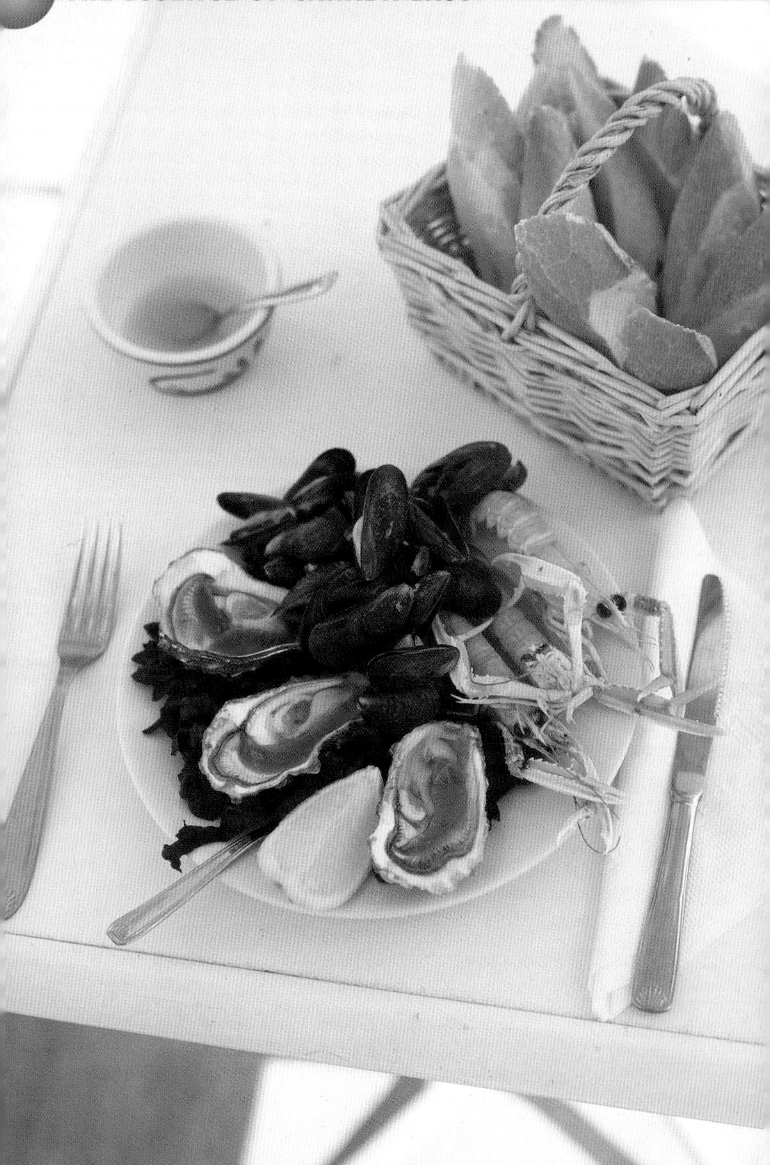

cider. The latter is delicious with foie gras, a side product of the ducks raised around Brome Lake, where thinly sliced *magret de canard* (duck breast) is a specialty. On Île d'Orléans, the Domaine Steinbach is one of several places in Québec making wonderful mustards.

In spring, a visit to a *cabane à sucre* (sugar shack) is fun. Celebrate the end of winter like a local by pouring maple syrup over everything – ham, beans, eggs, pancakes and so on. Wash it all down with a glass of caribou (a lethal mixture of brandy, vodka, sherry and port) or a kir (white wine and crème de cassis). And don't forget to try some maple taffy – hot maple syrup poured onto the snow and then eaten off a stick.

Popular with Québecois teenagers, and known as *poutine,* is a cholesterol-heavy mixture of French fries, cheese curds and gravy. You can even get the dish at McDonald's, and it has spread to the other eastern provinces too.

ONTARIO

The Niagara peninsula is a famous wine-making area that is also known for its ice wine, made with grapes that have frozen on the vine. It is quite sweet and rather expensive. There's lots of fresh produce here too – peaches, cherries, apricots and so on – as well as delicious jams.

Toronto has excellent restaurants known for their "fusion cuisine," but it's also a center for ethnic food from every corner of the world. Try visiting Kensington Market on a Saturday (► 162–163) or the St. Lawrence Market in Toronto for a peameal bacon sandwich (► 184). Canadian Club Whisky has been made in Walkerville (Windsor) for more than 150 years. It's lighter than scotch, smoother than bourbon, and is a great accompaniment to Canadian cheddar cheese made in Ingersoll.

short break

If you only have a short time to visit Eastern Canada and would like to take home some unforgettable memories try doing something that captures the real flavor of the region. The following suggestions feature classic sights and experiences that won't cost very much and will make your visit very special.

● **Drive the Cabot Trail** (➤ 70) through the Cape Breton Highlands National Park (➤ 38–39) to experience the most breathtaking scenery on one of the most beautiful islands in the world.

● **Take the boat trip** into Western Brook Pond in Gros Morne National Park (➤ 95) to wonder at this spectacular and deserted fjord, which is 16km (10 miles) long, 3km (2 miles) wide and 160m (525ft) deep.

● **Enjoy a lobster supper** on Prince Edward Island (➤ 100–101).

● **Picnic on the slopes of the Citadelle** in Québec City (➤ 127) on a summer evening and watch the sun set across the St. Lawrence River.

● **Order a beer** (or a *café au lait,* if it's early in the day) at one of the cafés on place Jacques Cartier (➤ 122) in Montréal and watch the world walk by, or be entertained by the street performers.

● **Take a jet-boat trip up the St. Lawrence** to the Lachine Rapids near Montréal and get soaked by the spray (or, for the adventurous, raft down the same rapids).

● **Visit Kensington Market** in Toronto (► 162–163) on a Saturday afternoon, when it is at its busiest, to experience the city's amazing ethnic diversity.

● **Go to the top of the CN Tower** (► 40–41) – after all, at 553.33m (1,815ft 5in), it is the world's tallest free-standing building!

● **Skate the length of the Rideau Canal** in Ottawa (➤ 157) in February, especially at the end of the day to watch the civil servants skating home from work as the sun sets.

● **Stand on the brink of the Niagara Falls** (➤ 44–45) and be mesmerized by the falling water. You may even forget the crowds – 14 million people visit the falls every year!

Planning

Before you go

WHEN TO GO

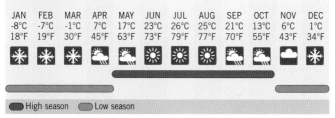

JAN	FEB	MAR	APR	MAY	JUN	JUL	AUG	SEP	OCT	NOV	DEC
-8°C	-7°C	-1°C	7°C	17°C	23°C	26°C	25°C	21°C	13°C	6°C	1°C
18°F	19°F	30°F	45°F	63°F	73°F	79°F	77°F	70°F	55°F	43°F	34°F

High season   Low season

Mostly, summers are warm and can actually get hot – in southern Ontario temperatures often reach 30°C (86°F) and humidity makes these days uncomfortable. It's fresher in coastal areas, and can be just as warm, though rain and fog are often seen; coastal winters are often milder than in much of Canada, but all regions get a great deal of snow.

WHAT YOU NEED

- ● Required
- ○ Suggested
- ▲ Not required

Some countries require a passport to remain valid for a minimum period (usually at least six months) beyond the date of entry – contact their consulate or embassy or your travel agent for details.

	UK	Germany	USA	France	Spain
Passport (or other acceptable form of ID)	●	●	●	●	●
Visa (regulations can change – check before you travel)	▲	▲	▲	▲	●
Onward or Return Ticket	○	○	○	○	○
Health Innoculations (tetanus and polio)	▲	▲	▲	▲	▲
Travel Insurance	○	○	○	○	○
Driving License (national)	●	●	●	●	●
Car Insurance Certificate	●	●	●	●	●
Car Registration Document	●	●	●	●	●

WEBSITES

- http://canada.gc.ca
- http://canadainternational.gc.ca
- www.pc.gc.ca
- www.canada.travel

TOURIST OFFICES

In the U.S.A. Canadian Tourism Commission, Yvonne Nichie (New York) ☎ 212/689-9307
Kristine Sigurdson (Los Angeles) ☎ 310/643-7768

In the U.K. Canadian Tourism Commission ✉ Visit Canada, PO Box 101, Chard TA20 9AR ☎ (0870) 380 0070

In Australia Canadian Tourism Commission ✉ Suite 105, Jones Bay Wharf, 26–32 Pirrama Road, Pyrmont, NSW 2009 ☎ (02) 9571 1665; fax: (02) 9571 1766

HEALTH INSURANCE

Visitors requiring treatment while in Canada must pay for it, which can be expensive. It is essential to take out health insurance. Make sure you keep all receipts to make a claim. Also ensure your coverage includes a "repatriation" clause in case no suitable treatment is available.

If you require dental help (expensive), ask at the reception desk of your hotel. Most hotels have a list of dentists.

TIME DIFFERENCES

| Ottawa (EST) 12 noon | New York 12 noon | Los Angeles 9AM | London 5PM | Tokyo 2AM | Sydney 5AM |

Eastern Canada has four different time zones. Most of Ontario and Québec observe Eastern Standard Time (EST). The most westerly part of Ontario observes Central Standard Time (EST -1). New Brunswick, Nova Scotia, Prince Edward Island, Labrador, and part of eastern Québec observe Atlantic Standard Time (EST +1). The island of Newfoundland observes Newfoundland Standard Time (1.5 hours ahead of EST). Daylight Saving Time (DST) is observed from mid-March to early November.

NATIONAL AND PROVINCIAL HOLIDAYS

Jan 1 *New Year's Day*

Mar 17 *St. Patrick's Day* (Newfoundland and Labrador)

Mar–Apr *Good Friday*

Mar–Apr *Easter Monday*

Apr 23 *St. George's Day* (Newfoundland and Labrador)

May (Mon closest to 24) *Victoria Day*

Jun 24 *St-Jean-Baptiste Day* (Québec)

Jun 24 *Discovery Day* (Newfoundland and Labrador)

Jul 1 *Canada Day*

Jul 12 *Orangeman's Day* (Newfoundland and Labrador)

Aug (1st Mon) *New Brunswick Day* (New Brunswick)

Aug (1st Mon) *Civic holiday* (Ontario)

Aug (1st Mon) *Natal Day* (Nova Scotia, except in Halifax, usually Jul or Aug)

Aug (1st Mon) *Natal Day* (PEI – by proclamation)

Aug *Regatta Day/civic holiday* (Newfoundland and Labrador – fixed by municipal council orders)

Sep (1st Mon) *Labour Day*

Oct (2nd Mon) *Thanksgiving* (note: this is not at the same time as American Thanksgiving)

Nov 11 *Remembrance Day* (not celebrated in Québec)

Dec 25 *Christmas Day*

Dec 26 *Boxing Day*

WHAT'S ON WHEN
Festival Nation

The festivals and events listed here are the best-known and most established in Eastern Canada, for example, Canada Day on July 1 is universally celebrated. Almost every community organizes some kind of celebration during the summer months so it's worthwhile inquiring locally during your visit.

January/February

Niagara Icewine Celebrations, Niagara Peninsula *WinterCity*, Toronto

Québec Winter Carnival (➤ 60), Québec City

Winterlude, Ottawa

Montréal High Lights Festival, Montréal
March *SnoBreak Winter Festival,* Goose Bay, Labrador
Toronto Canada Blooms: Flower and Garden Show, Toronto
April *Blue Metropolis Literary Festival,* Montréal
World Stage International Theatre Festival, Toronto
May *Santé: International Wine Festival,* Toronto
Canadian Tulip Festival (➤ 60), Ottawa
June *Canada Dance Festival,* Ottawa
June/July *Festival 500 – Sharing the Voices* (➤ 60), St. John's (odd numbered years)
Nova Scotia International Tattoo, Halifax
Charlottetown Festival, Prince Edward Island
International Jazz Festival (➤ 60), Montréal
Montréal International Fireworks Competition, Montréal
July *Canada's Irish Festival,* Miramichi, New Brunswick
Just for Laughs Comedy Festival (➤ 60), Montréal
Festival d'été du Québec, Québec City
Les Grands Feux Loto Québec, Montmorency, Québec
Festival de Lanaudière, Joliette, Québec (July–August, dates vary year to year)
Divers/Cité – International Gay & Lesbian Pride Festival, Montréal (July–August, dates vary year to year)
Kingston Buskers Rendezvous, Kingston
August *Halifax International Busker Festival,* Halifax
Atlantic Seafood Festival (➤ 60), Moncton, New Brunswick
Fergus Scottish Festival and Highland Games, Fergus, Ontario
Festival of the Islands, Gananoque, Ontario
Canadian National Exhibition (➤ 60), Toronto (18 August–4 September)
Canadian Grand Masters Fiddle Championship, Nepean, Ottawa
September *Toronto International Film Festival,* Toronto
Harvest Jazz and Blues Festival, Fredericton
Niagara Wine Festival, St. Catharines, Ontario
October *Celtic Colours International Festival,* Sydney, Cape Breton, Nova Scotia
Oktoberfest (➤ 60), Kitchener, Ontario
November *Canadian Aboriginal Festival,* Toronto
December *Christmas Lights Across Canada* (➤ 60), Ottawa

Getting there

BY AIR

Toronto International Airport

27km (17 miles) from city center

🚖 45 minutes

🚌 45 minutes

🚐 1–1.5 hours

Montréal International Airport

14.5km (9 miles) from city center

🚖 30 minutes

🚌 30 minutes

Eastern Canada's major airports are in Toronto (Toronto Lester B. Pearson International Airport; www.gtaa.com) and Montréal (Montréal-Pierre Elliott Trudeau International Airport; www.admtl.com); most visitors arrive at one or the other. There are smaller airports in Ottawa, Québec, Halifax and St. John's. The major Canadian airline is Air Canada tel: 888/247-2262 (toll free); www.aircanada.com.

Toronto's airport, Canada's largest, is 27km (17 miles) northwest of the city center. The Airport Express Bus (www.torontoairportexpress.com) to downtown hotels and the bus station runs regularly about every 30 minutes (every 20 minutes during peak times) and takes roughly 45 minutes. A cheaper option is the regular transit bus (www.ttc.ca). The Montréal-Pierre Elliott Trudeau International Airport is just 14.5km (9 miles) from downtown and L'Aérobus shuttle (www.autobus.qc.ca) runs to the bus station.

DRIVING

- Drive on the right, pass on the left.
- You can turn right at red lights, after stopping to check that the way is clear, unless otherwise signed. However, this is illegal in Montréal.
- Speed limits on highways: 100kph (60mph) or 110kph (68mph)
  Speed limits on other major roads: 70–80kph (40–50mph)
  Speed limits in urban areas and on rural routes: 50kph (30mph) or less.
- Seat belts must be worn by all people in a vehicle (drivers and passengers) in both the front and back seats and child safety seats are a legal requirement.
- Random breath-testing. Never drive under the influence of alcohol.
- Gasoline is heavily taxed. Gas stations stay open until 9–10pm (some all night). Away from the much-traveled south, gas stations may be far apart and close at 8pm.
- If you intend to drive long distances in remote areas, take out membership in the Canadian Automobile Association (www.caa.ca; South Central Ontario tel: 800/268-3750, www.caasco.on.ca; North and East Ontario tel:1-800/267-8713, www.caaneo.com; Niagara tel: 905/984-8585, www.caaniagara.net; Québec tel:1-800/686-9243, www.caaquebec.com; Maritimes tel:1-800/561-8807, www.caa.maritimes.ca). They or their local affiliate can help in case of breaking down.
- If you are a member of AAA, you are entitled to full service with the CAA if you have your membership card with you.

Getting around

PUBLIC TRANSPORTATION
Internal flights

Air Canada (tel: 888/247-2262 toll free; www.aircanada.ca) subsidiary Air Canada Jazz (www.flyjazz.ca) is the region's major carrier. WestJet (tel: 888/937-8538 toll free; www.westjet.com) offers services across Canada and some U.S. destinations. Air Labrador (tel: 800/563-3042; www.airlabrador.com) links remote Newfoundland and Labrador destinations with Montréal, Québec City and other east-coast airports. First Air (tel: 800/267-1247; www.firstair.ca) provides links from Ottawa or Montréal with the far north.

Trains

VIA Rail (tel: 888/842-7245 toll free; www.viarail.ca) provides most rail passenger services in Eastern Canada. There are excellent daily services between Montréal and Toronto, Montréal and Québec, and Montréal and Ottawa. Trains run several times a week between Montréal and Gaspé, and Montréal and Halifax.

Buses

Long-distance buses This is the least expensive option and gives access to most of the region. Greyhound Canada (tel: 800/661-8747 toll free; www.greyhound.ca) serves Ontario, Québec, New Brunswick and Nova Scotia with cross-border links to U.S. cities.

Ferries In Nova Scotia, services link Yarmouth with the state of Maine, Digby with Saint John, New Brunswick, and Caribou with Wood

Islands, Prince Edward Island. The Nova Scotia Tourist Office can supply details. Newfoundland is linked to North Sydney, Nova Scotia, by two different ferries run by Marine Atlantic (www.marine-atlantic.ca).

Urban transportation Toronto and Montréal have excellent subway systems. The Toronto Transit System (TTC tel: 416/393-4636; www.ttc.ca), operates buses, streetcars, the subway and a light rapid transit system (LTR). The Société de Transport de Montréal (STM tel: 514/786-4636; www.stm.info), runs the métro and bus service.

TAXIS

Taxis are the most expensive option. Fares mount quickly, especially in rush-hour traffic. Cabs can be found in stands beside major hotels, at airports and at train and bus stations or can be hailed on the street or called by telephone.

CAR RENTAL

All the major car-rental companies are represented in Eastern Canada (Avis, Budget, Dollar, Hertz, National, and Thrifty). You must be over 21, and produce identification and a valid driver's license (which you have held for at least a year).

FARES AND TICKETS

Tickets for flights, train and buses can be bought online as well as at airports, stations and ticket agents. Long-distance bus and train companies also offer passes covering various periods of unlimited travel. In Toronto, free transfers are available for continuing your journey by bus or streetcar, but must be obtained when paying the subway fare. Bus fares can be paid in cash to the driver, but you need the exact fare.

Reduced rates are available for children, students and seniors (proof of age or status required). Most museums, galleries and tourist attractions offer concessions and there are often combined ticket deals covering more than one attraction in a town or city.

Being there

TOURIST OFFICES

● **Tourism New Brunswick**
✉ P.O. Box 12345, Campbellton, New Brunswick, E3N 3T6
☎ 800/561-0123 (toll free); www.tourismnewbrunswick.ca

● **Newfoundland and Labrador Department of Tourism**
✉ P.O. Box 8700, St. John's, Newfoundland and Labrador, A1B 4J6 ☎ 800/563-6353 (toll free); www.newfoundland labrador.com

● **Nova Scotia Tourism**
✉ P.O. Box 456, Halifax, Nova Scotia, B3J 2R5 ☎ 800/565-0000 (toll free); www.novascotia.com

● **Ontario Travel**
✉ 10th Floor, Hearst Block, 900 Bay Street, Toronto, Ontario, M7A 2E1 ☎ 800/668-2746 (toll free); www.ontariotravel.net

● **Prince Edward Island Department of Tourism**
✉ P.O. Box 940, Charlottetown, Prince Edward Island, C1A 7M5
☎ 800/463-4734 (toll free); www.gov.pe.ca/visitorsguide

● **Tourisme Québec**
✉ P.O. Box 979, Montréal, Québec, H3C 2W3 ☎ 877/266-5687 (toll free); www.bonjourquebec.com

MONEY

Eastern Canada's currency is the Canadian dollar (1 dollar = 100 cents). There are $5, $10, $20, $50 and $100 bills (notorious for forgeries and can be difficult to use). Coins come as pennies (1 cent), nickels (5 cents), dimes (10 cents), quarters (25 cents), loonies ($1, so called because of the bird on them), and twonies ($2). U.S. dollars are widely accepted, but stores, restaurants, etc. might not offer the best exchange rate.

TIPS/GRATUITIES

Yes ✓ No ✗		
Restaurants (if service not included)	✓	10–15%
Cafés	✓	10%
Taxis	✓	10–15%
Porters	✓	$1–$2/bag
Chambermaids	✓	$2–$5/week
Washrooms/restrooms	✗	
Tour guides	✓	$1

POSTAL AND INTERNET SERVICES

Mail boxes are generally red, with the words "Canada Post" or "Postes Canada" written on them. For hours of post offices, ➤ 32. For more information visit www.canadapost.ca.

In all major towns and cities, internet access is available at libraries and internet cafés. There are WiFi hotspots in Montréal, Halifax, Ottawa, Toronto, and several other towns and cities in Ontario. Many hotels offer internet access, sometimes free but usually for a charge.

TELEPHONES

Outdoor public telephones are located in glass and metal booths. To make a call, lift the handset, insert the correct coin (25¢ or $1), a telephone credit card or a prepaid calling card, probably the most convenient means to make a long-distance call (available from post offices, convenience stores and newsagents), then dial.

In Toronto and Montréal include the area code, even when dialling from within the city. The toll-free numbers listed in this guide are free only when calling from within North America.

Emergency telephone numbers
Police, Fire, Ambulance: 911
(except in Prince Edward Island and Nova Scotia where you dial 0 for the operator).

International dialling codes
From Canada to:
U.S.A. 1
U.K. 011 44
France 011 33

EMBASSIES AND CONSULATES

U.S.A. ☎ 613/688-5335;
www.usembassy.gov
U.K. ☎ 613/237-1530;
http://ukincanada.fco.gov.uk/en/
Australia ☎ 613/236-0841;
www.ahc-ottawa.org

France ☎ 613/789-1795;
www.ambafrance-ca.org
Germany ☎ 613/232-1101;
www.ottawa.diplo.de

ELECTRICITY

The voltage across Eastern Canada is 110 volts, the same as in the U.S.A. Sockets require plugs with two (or three) flat prongs. Visitors from outside North America will require an adapter as well as a voltage converter.

HEALTH AND SAFETY

Sun advice In Ontario and Québec temperatures can reach the 30s °C (80s and 90s °F) so use sunscreen. Winter sun reflected off snow can cause serious sunburn so use sunscreen during outdoor activities.

Prescription drugs Over-the-counter drugs are readily available in pharmacies but out-of-province prescriptions are never accepted. If you run out of medication get a new prescription from a local doctor.

Safe water Tap water is perfectly safe to drink. When camping, boil drinking water to protect yourself against "beaver fever."

Pretty crime Although crime rates are low in Eastern Canada you should still take precautions:

- Don't leave bags or other valuables visible in your car.
- Don't wear expensive jewelry or carry large sums of money.
- In the major cities consider carrying your passport and credit cards in a pouch or belt.
- Keep to well-lit streets at night.

The Royal Canadian Mounted Police (RCMP; www.rcmp-grc.gc.ca) is the federal police force. When on duty they look like any other police force and drive cars – the famous uniform and horses are used for ceremonies.

OPENING HOURS

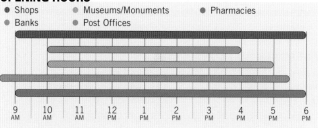

- Shops
- Banks
- Museums/Monuments
- Post Offices
- Pharmacies

Most stores open Mon–Wed 9–6, Thu–Fri 9–9, Sat 9–5, Sun noon–5 although supermarkets and shopping malls often have longer hours.
Banks open Mon–Fri 9:30–4 but some close at 5pm or 6pm on Thu or Fri.
Post offices are open Mon–Fri 8:30–5:30 (sometimes later) and Sat am.
Museums open Tue–Sun 10–5 with art museums often opening at 11.
Most are closed Mon and some stay open until 9 one evening a week.

LANGUAGE

The official language of the province of Québec is French and New Brunswick is officially bilingual. Most Québec sights in the book are listed by their French name, followed by the English translation. For a few sights the English name is given first when this is in common use.

hello	*bonjour*	please	*s'il vous plaît*
good evening	*bonsoir*	Excuse me	*Excusez-moi*
good night	*bon nuit*	How much?	*Combien?*
goodbye	*au revoir*	open/closed	*ouvert/fermé*
yes/no	*oui/non*	Where is..?	*Où est..?*
thank you	*merci*	morning/afternoon	*matin/après-midi*
you're welcome	*bienvenue*	evening/night	*soir/nuit*
hotel/inn	*hôtel/auberge*	double room	*occupation double*
bed-and-breakfast	*gîte touristique*	one night	*une nuit*
single room	*occupation simple*	room service	*service à la chambre*
bank	*banque*	banknote	*billet de banque*
exchange office	*bureau de change*	check	*chèque*
post office	*bureau de poste*	traveler's check	*chèque de voyage*
coin	*pièce de monnaie*	credit card	*carte de credit*
restaurant	*restaurant*	menu	*menu/table d'hôte*
café	*café*	waiter	*serveur*
pub/bar	*brasserie/bar*	The check, please	*L'addition s'il vous plaît*
breakfast/lunch/ dinner	*déjeuner/dîner/ souper*	washrooms/ restrooms	*toilettes*
table	*table*		
airport/airplane	*aéroport/avion*	subway/bus/taxi	*métro/autobus/taxi*
ferry/port	*traversier/port*	station/train/tickets	*gare/train/billets*
customs/ international border	*douanes/ frontière*	entrance/exit	*entrée/sortie*
		right/left	*droite/gauche*
		straight ahead	*tout droit*
expressway/ road/street	*autoroute/ chemin/rue*	north/south/ east/west	*nord/sud/ est/ouest*

Best places to see

1 Canadian Museum of Civilization, Gatineau

www.civilization.ca

Their curved lines evoking the birth of the North American continent, the buildings of the Canadian Museum of Civilization are stunning, quite the most interesting architectural ensemble in Canada.

The Canadian Museum of Civilization occupies a fine site across the Ottawa River from the Canadian Parliament Buildings (► 156). The masterpiece of architect Douglas Cardinal, opened in 1989, the buildings suggest the emergence of man on a continent sculpted and eroded by nature. Even the Manitoba limestone cladding is significant, with its fossils dating back from early geological times. The less dramatic structure is the curatorial block. The museum proper is characterized by large glass walls and huge copper vaults and domes.

The Great Hall forms the museum's architectural centerpiece, occupying a whopping 1,782sq m (19,182sq ft) of space and with floor-to-ceiling windows rising 112m (365ft). It houses six complete log houses of the Pacific coast peoples set along a shoreline, and includes a magnificent collection of totem poles. A large contemporary sculpture by Bill Reid hangs at the far end. Called *Spirit of Haida Gwaii*, this original plaster shows a Haida canoe full of people paddling vigorously.

Under a vast domed ceiling, the Canada Hall features full-scale buildings in which real-life characters bring alive a panorama of Canadian history. Highlights include a Basque whaling station, a town square from New France and an early Loyalist settlement in Ontario. The newest gallery, Face to Face, explores the lives of people who have significantly contributed to Canadian history.

✚ 8D ✉ 100 Laurier Street, P.O. Box 3100, Station B, Gatineau, Québec, KIA 0M8. The museum is easily accessible from Ottawa (Ontario) by bridge ☎ 819/776-7000; 800/555-5621 (toll free) 🕔 Daily (closed Mon mid-Oct to Apr) 💷 Expensive; free Thu 4–9. Parking charge 🍴 Restaurant ($$$), cafeteria ($), café ($) ❓ Guided tours. Craft boutique, IMAX movie theater, Children's Museum, Postal Musuem

2 Cape Breton Highlands National Park

Stunning scenery of forest-clad mountains plunging down to a rocky coastline dotted with delightful bays and beaches makes this one of the most beautiful national parks in Canada.

On the northernmost tip of Nova Scotia, Cape Breton frequently features prominently on lists of the most beautiful islands in the world. The area that is preserved as the national park stretches from coast to coast just short of its northern-most tip and consists of 950sq km (366sq miles) of densely forested, rugged wilderness.

That's not to say it is inaccessible. Scenic Highway 19 – better known as the Cabot Trail (➤ 16, 70) – forms a convenient horseshoe along the coastlines and across the top of the park, with regular pull-offs for safe parking and access to the 25 trails that lead into the interior or down to secluded coves. These range from short but fascinating "leg-stretchers" to the challenging Fishing Cove hike of

more than 15km (10 miles) from the top of MacKenzie Mountain to sea level and back. All are designed to explore this complex environment, which encompasses southern and arctic plants, and woodland that provides spectacular fall colors. The forests are home to some 40 species of mammals, including moose, coyote and lynx, and the offshore marine environment has whales, seals and a variety of seabirds. Whale-watching trips operate from Chéticamp, Pleasant Bay and Ingonish.

Check the weather before a visit – sea mists often roll in and mar the view – and try to make a first call at the excellent park center just north of Chéticamp, where there is an audio-visual program, hands-on exhibits, kids' activities, maps and information.

✚ 21J ✉ Parks Canada, Ingonish Beach, Nova Scotia B0C 1L0 ☎ 902/224-2306; www.pc.gc.ca/pnnp/ns/cbreton/ 🕐 Park: daily; information center: mid-May to mid-Oct daily 9–5 (8–8 in summer) ✋ Moderate (visitors need to buy a permit)

🍴 Restaurants and cafés at Chéticamp, Pleasant Bay and Ingonish ($–$$)

Chéticamp Information Centre

✉ Highway 19, north of Chéticamp
☎ 902/224-2306 🕐 Mid-May to mid-Oct daily 9–5 (8–8 in summer)

3 CN Tower, Toronto

www.cntower.ca

The ultimate symbol of modern Toronto, this needle-thin mast with a bulge two-thirds of the way up was the world's tallest building until a Dubai hotel eclipsed it in 2007. The view from it is nothing short of spectacular.

The CN Tower rises an incredible 553.33m (1,815ft 5in). Love it or hate it, there's no denying that it has enhanced Toronto's skyline ever since its construction in the 1970s. Glass-fronted elevators climb to the Look Out, two-thirds of the way up

(346m, or 1,136ft, above the ground) at a stomach-churning speed of 6m (20ft) a second. The city's landmarks can easily be identified either from inside or from an outdoor observatory one floor down. Those with a good head for heights can even look directly down at the ground while standing on a glass floor.

Don't miss the ascent to the SkyPod, another 33 floors up, or 447m (1,465ft) above the ground. This is the world's highest man-made observatory and the view is superb. Visibility can exceed 160km (100 miles) and, with luck, you will be able to make out the spray of Niagara Falls and the city of Rochester, New York state, across Lake Ontario. You should be aware, however, that the tower can sway up to 1.8m (6ft) from the vertical on windy days – a normal but somewhat unnerving sensation.

The CN Tower was not primarily intended as a tourist attraction, but a telecommunications tower. During the 1960s, Toronto experienced a construction boom that transformed the skyline from one characterized by relatively low buildings, into one dotted with skyscrapers. These new buildings caused serious communications problems as they got in the way of the airwaves. However, the CN Tower, with microwave receptors at 338m (1,109ft) and topped by an antenna, effectively solved these difficulties.

✚ *Toronto 2b* ✉ 301 Front Street, Toronto, Ontario, M5V 2T6 ☎ 416/868-6937 🕐 Daily; closed Dec 25; hours of operation adjusted seasonally 💰 Expensive 🍴 360 Restaurant ($$$), cafés ($) 🚇 Union Station ❓ Souvenir shops. Long lines during peak times and seasons

4 Mont-Royal, Montréal

www.lemontroyal.qc.ca

Mont-Royal Park, the jewel in Montréal's crown, was created by the landscape architect Frederick Law Olmstead, and offers magnificent views of the city and river from its Chalet viewpoint.

At the center of the island of Montréal and deep in the heart of the city, the bulky lump of Mont-Royal rises 228m (750ft). "La Montagne" (the Mountain) is not only a lovely park, but it is also part of the city's soul. It provides a wonderful oasis of greenery in the center of the bustling metropolis, and as such is popular with residents year-round.

In 1876, the city expropriated the land at the top of the mountain for a hefty $1 million, and then invited Frederick Law Olmstead (famous for designing Central Park in New York) to landscape it. Near the summit, the large stone Smith House, built in 1858, acts as a visitors' centre, with an exhibition about the park and a café.

High above the bustle of the city, the Chalet offers views that are nothing less than spectacular. The downtown highrises are particularly prominent. The mighty St. Lawrence can be seen winding its way around the city, and on clear days the Adirondack Mountains of northern New York state are visible, as are the Green Mountains of Vermont. The view is equally spectacular at night.

The wide, flat St. Lawrence valley is punctuated by a series of small, rather dramatic peaks like Mont-Royal, which were created about 60 million years ago during a period of tectonic activity. These igneous plugs are known as the Collines Montérégiennes (Monteregian Hills), from *mons regius*, the Latin name for Mont-Royal. According to most historians, the city's name also derives from Mont-Royal.

✚ *Montréal 1e (off map)*
✉ Parc du Mont-Royal, Voie Camillien-Houde, Montréal, Québec ☎ 514/843-8240
🕐 Daily 🚶 Free; parking charge 🍴 Cafeteria ($) at Smith House 🚌 11 from Mont-Royal métro station and rue Côte-des-Nieges ❓ Accessible on foot from avenue du Parc, avenue des Pins, and rue Côte-des-Nieges via Trafalgar staircase (200 steps; allow 20 mins)

5 Niagara Falls

www.niagaraparks.com

In 1678, French explorer Louis Hennepin exclaimed, "The universe does not afford its parallel," a sentiment still echoed by the millions of people who flock to Niagara Falls every year.

This famous waterfall is one of the best-known, most visited and most photographed sights in the world. Around 14 million people visit it annually, taking an estimated 100 million photographs. The fascination of watching all that "thundering water" (the meaning of the First Nations word Niagara) endlessly flowing over the rock edge has a totally mesmerizing effect. Few are disappointed; many are more impressed than they expected to be. Niagara Falls are quite simply fantastic.

Just before it reaches tiny Goat Island, the Niagara River divides into two. About 10 percent of the water heads for the American Falls (so called because they are on the U.S. side of the river), which are more than 300m (985ft) wide and 54m (176ft) high. The rest of the water heads for the Canadian, or Horseshoe Falls, which are named for their shape and are nearly 800m (2,625ft) wide and about 51m (167ft) high. The water crashes over the falls at the incredible rate of 155 million liters (40 million gallons) per minute.

At Table Rock, you can approach the very edge of the Horseshoe Falls, the point where the tumultuous water plunges over the cliff. It is incredibly impressive, but it can also be wet on windy days. From here you can descend by elevator

to two outdoor observation decks directly behind the falls – also impressive and wet. And nobody should miss the exciting (and wet) *Maid of the Mist* boat trip.

✚ 8B ✉ Niagara Parks Commission ☎ 905/371-0254; 877/642-7275 ✋ Parking: expensive. Boat tour: expensive ❚❙ Elements on the Falls Restaurant ($$$), cafés ($) 🚌 People Mover bus: daily, Mar–Dec 🚢 *Maid of the Mist*: daily, late Apr or early May–late Oct; Niagara Parkway (▶ 173) ❓ Welcome Centers are located at Table Rock, *Maid of the Mist* ticket booth and various locations

Rocher Percé, Gaspésie

www.rocherperce.com

A massive pierced limestone rock sits seemingly at anchor just off the tiny community of Percé at the end of the magnificent Gaspé Peninsula.

Rocher Percé is a limestone block formed from layers of sediment deposited on the seabed about 375 million years ago. It soars high above the surrounding sand to 88m (289ft) and is an amazing 438m (1,437ft) in length. At its eastern end, it is pierced by an arch. Once there were two arches here, but in 1848, during a storm, one collapsed to leave the separate pinnacle now known as the Obelisk.

Renowned for the beauty of its site, the village of Percé is blessed with a varied topography, and nowhere else on the peninsula are the geological forces that shaped Gaspésie more evident. Yellowish limestone and red conglomerate rock have been squeezed, folded and manipulated into an incredible variety of protruding cliffs, deep bays and craggy hills.

You can park in the town and walk out to Rocher Percé – or even around it if the tide is out. Every cape and headland in the community offers a different view. Mont-Ste.-Anne, the craggy peak dominating the town, has particularly splendid panoramas, although the path leading up it is steep (the trail begins beside the church; allow 1.5 hours to reach the summit). You get another wonderful view of Rocher Percé by taking the boat tour to Bonaventure Island, which passes close to the rock before making a circular tour of the island famous for its seabirds, notably its huge gannet colony.

✚ 20J ⅱ Variety of restaurants and cafés in Percé ? Boat tours in summer only (details available from tourist information office) ⓘ Information touristique de Percé: 142 Route 132, Percé, Québec, G0C 2L0 ☎ 418/782-5448

7

Science North, Sudbury

www.sciencenorth.on.ca

Set in an oval crater in the Precambrian Canadian Shield, Sudbury is home to a stunning science center hewn out of the rock below two glittering snowflake-shaped buildings.

Even if you find science the most boring thing on Earth, you will be impressed by Science North, in Sudbury, deep in northern Ontario's mining belt. The two unusual snowflake buildings, representing the glaciation that sculpted the Canadian landscape, are clad with stainless steel, the main ingredient of which is locally mined nickel.

An underground rock tunnel links the two buildings, ending in a huge underground cavern representing the crater in which the center sits. From the cavern, visitors proceed to the exhibit floors along a glass-enclosed ramp that offers views of Ramsey Lake and part of a fault that runs through the rock at this point. This rock fault was deliberately excavated for its geological interest.

As far as the exhibits are concerned, you have to roll up your sleeves and get involved. You can have a go at building a robot in the LEGO Mindstorms Robotics Lab, and if that doesn't appeal, you can hold a snake or watch beavers in action. WaterWorks: Soak Up the Science! is a new exhibit all about H2O, from making a rainbow to learning about water power through interactive games. There are also laser shows and IMAX

movies; the Virtual Voyages Adventure Ride, and a
tropical greenhouse where 400 tropical butterflies
fly free. An offshoot museum, Dynamic Earth
(➤ 176), also injects fun into geology and mining.

✚ 6C ✉ 100 Ramsey Lake Road, Sudbury, Ontario, P3E
5S9 ☎ 705/522-3701; 800/461-4898 (toll free) ⏰ Daily
✋ Expensive 🍴 Restaurant ($$), cafeteria ($), food court
($) ⛴ Boat cruises on Ramsey Lake ❓ Whizards Gift Store

8 Signal Hill, St. John's

www.pc.gc.ca

The Newfoundland capital has a spectacular site on the slopes of a natural harbor whose narrow entrance is guarded by the great rock of Signal Hill.

No visit to St. John's would be complete without a climb up Signal Hill for panoramic views of the city, harbor and coastline. A calm day is best for the excursion – if there is even a light breeze in the city, the wind will be strong on Signal Hill. The cliffs rise sharply to form this rocky outcrop facing the Atlantic Ocean. At the top stands Cabot Tower, the city's best-known landmark, built in 1897 to commemorate the 400th anniversary of John Cabot's visit to Newfoundland. From here, you can look straight down into The Narrows, the 200m wide (650ft) entrance to the harbor, while to the southeast is Cape Spear, North America's most easterly point.

As its name suggests, Signal Hill has long been used for signalling. From the early 18th century, flags were flown from its summit to alert local merchants to the approach of their vessels. In 1901, a different type of communication took place when Guglielmo Marconi received the first transatlantic wireless signal from Poldhu in Cornwall, England. That letter "s" in Morse code traversed more than 2,700km (1,700 miles) to make history.

Today a national historic park, Signal Hill has a visitor center and a great trail system. From Cabot Tower, you can walk over to Queen's Battery or to Ladies Lookout at 160m (525ft). Avid hikers can descend the North Head to The Narrows via a steep trail on the ocean side.

✚ 23L ✉ Signal Hill Road, St. John's, Newfoundland and Labrador, A1C 5M9 ☎ 709/772-5367 🕓 Daily. Visitor center: mid-May to mid-Oct daily 8:30–8; mid-Oct to mid-May Mon–Fri 8:30–4:30 💲 Signal Hill: free. Visitor center: inexpensive 🍴 Picnic facilities ❓ Military drills are performed by cadets Jul–Aug. Gift shop in Cabot Tower

9 Terrasse Dufferin and Promenade des Gouverneurs, Québec City

Admiring the city from the Dufferin Terrace and then following the spectacular Governors' Walk as it clings to the cliff face is one of the glories of a visit to Québec.

The Terrasse Dufferin (Dufferin Terrace) is a wide wooden boardwalk suspended high above the St. Lawrence River, offering magnificent views over the surrounding country. Extending for a total of 670m (2,200ft), it is popular year-round, day and night. On summer evenings, there are street performers, while in the winter, you can try the toboggan slide.

The history of Terrasse Dufferin starts in 1620 with Samuel de Champlain, whose statue stands in front of the Château Frontenac. He constructed the Château St. Louis here, which served as the residence of first the French, and later the British governors until it was destroyed by fire in 1834. At that time, the British governor, Lord Durham, built a platform over the ruins and allowed public access. The structure was then extended on a couple of occasions, notably in 1879 by Governor General Lord Dufferin, whose name it commemorates.

From the terrace's southern end, and accessed by a steep flight of stairs, a spectacular boardwalk

inaugurated in 1960 clings to the cliff about 90m (300ft) above the river. This is the Promenade des Gouverneurs (Governors' Walk), which goes around the outer walls of the Citadelle (➤ 127) with splendid views of the St. Lawrence, the Basse-Ville (Lower Town), Île d'Orléans and the opposite shore of the river as far as the mountains of northern Maine on a clear day. If you don't mind climbing its 310 steps, it provides an excellent means of getting to the Plains of Abraham, site of the decisive battle in the Seven Years' War.

✚ 10E ⊙ Terrasse Dufferin: daily. Promenade des Gouverneurs: May–Oct daily ✋ Free 🍴 Restaurants and cafés nearby ❓ Terrasse Dufferin adjoins place d'Armes in front of Château Frontenac. Promenade des Gouverneurs runs from the southern end of Terrasse Dufferin to avenue du Cap-Diamant in National Battlefields Park

10 Whale-watching, Tadoussac

The rich waters at the point where the Saguenay River joins the St. Lawrence have long attracted giant mammals of the deep, and have made Tadoussac a famous whale-watching center.

Every day, the salty tides of the St. Lawrence River sweep into the mouth of the Saguenay, and in its turn the main stream is invaded by the fresh waters of its tributary. This mixture of waters has created a rich ecosystem where plankton flourishes, and that draws in small creatures such as krill, shrimp and

capelin which, in their turn, attract larger predators. A resident population of about 500 beluga, or white whales, haunts these waters. Fin and minke whales are also frequently viewed off Tadoussac, and occasionally humpback whales are sighted.

Tadoussac has a fine site on the cliffs and sand dunes along the north shore of the St. Lawrence, but it is rare to spot whales from the shore. The St. Lawrence is more than 10km (6 miles) wide at this point, and it is mid-river, miles from shore, where the whales frolic, great jets of water issuing from their blowholes just before they surface.

In the summer, a procession of small boats leaves Tadoussac wharf, offering a variety of tours. The views of the town and the mouth of the Saguenay are magnificent. Standing on a shoal close to the intersection of these two important waterways is the Prince Light, a 15m-high (50ft) lighthouse that was constructed after the Prince of Wales' ship ran aground here in the 1880s.

✚ 18H 🖑 Expensive 🍴 Restaurants in Tadoussac

Croisières AML

✉ 124 rue St-Pierre, Québec City, Québec, G1K 4A7

☎ 418/692-2634; 800/563-4643 (toll free);

www.croisieresaml.com 🕐 May–Oct daily

Famille Dufour Croisières

✉ 22 quai St.-André, Québec City, Québec, G1K 9B7

☎ 418/692-0222; 800/463-5250 (toll free); www.dufour.ca

🕐 May–Oct daily

Best things to do

Good places to have lunch

Auberge Baker ($$$)
Traditional Québec food in an old French house between Québec City and Ste-Anne-de-Beaupré. Guests are seated either in the original section, dating from 1840, or a new, more airy addition. The menu offers both traditional and "contemporary" dishes.
✉ 8790 chemin Royale, Château-Richer, Québec ☎ 418/824-4478

Le Café du Château ($)
Great salads and light lunches in the Governor's Garden, Château Ramezay Museum, Old Montréal.
✉ 280 rue Notre-Dame Est, Montréal, Québec ☎ 514/861-1112
🕐 May–Sep only

Café l'Entrée ($)
Spectacular location in the Great Hall of the National Gallery of Canada; the menu emphasizes delicious, simply prepared foods.
✉ 380 Sussex Drive, Ottawa, Ontario ☎ 613/991-4060

Café-Restaurant du Musée ($$)
Excellent café in the Musée du Québec serving all-Québec produce; outdoor terrace in summer.
✉ Parc des Champs-de-Bataille, Québec City, Québec ☎ 418/644-6780

Cheapside Café ($)
Elegant café in the Art Gallery of Nova Scotia offering excellent light lunches and the chance to meet local politicians – the Legislature is across the street.
✉ 1723 Hollis Street, Halifax, Nova Scotia ☎ 902/424-7542

Chocolaterie and Patisserie Fackelman/The Schnitzel Parlor ($)
Beside the St. John River just west of the city, this cosy place serves hearty German food and irresistible desserts. Reservations are required.
✉ 2785 Woodstock Road, Fredericton, New Brunswick ☎ 506/450-2520

Lago Restaurant ($$)

Stylish place in Queen's Quay Terminal (➤ 72) with great food and wonderful views of the lake. Dine on the big lakeside patio or in the chic interior.

✉ 207 Queen's Quay West, Queen's Quay Terminal, Toronto, Ontario
☎ 416/848-0005

Lake House Restaurant ($$)

Simple, charming restaurant in Science North, overlooking Ramsey Lake. The menu is extensive and ranges from simple salads and sandwiches to filet mignon.

✉ 100 Ramsey Lake Road, Sudbury, Ontario ☎ 705/522-3701, ext. 505

Mavor's Bistro ($$)

Pleasant café with a long menu of bistro-style fare in the Confederation Centre of the Arts.

✉ 145 Richmond Street, Charlottetown, Prince Edward Island
☎ 902/628-6107

Restaurant Acadien ($)

Charming restaurant in the museum and craft shop serving Acadian specialties including meat pies and chowder, served by staff in traditional dress; on the Cabot Trail.

✉ 744 Main Street, Chéticamp, Cape Breton, Nova Scotia ☎ 902/224-3207

Annual events

Winter Carnival, Québec City: Parade, ice sculptures and canoe races across the ice-strewn St. Lawrence (Jan–Feb).

Canadian Tulip Festival, Ottawa: A rite of spring; more than 3 million tulips decorate the city (May).

Festival 500 – Sharing the Voices, St. John's, Newfoundland: International festival of choral singing, with choirs from all over the world (Jun/Jul).

International Jazz Festival, Montréal: More than 500 shows, 350 of them outdoors and free, in the heart of downtown Montréal (Jun/Jul).

Just for Laughs Comedy Festival, Montréal: 11 days of laughter, with top comedians and free outdoor shows (Jul).

Royal Nova Scotia International Tattoo, Halifax: Pipe bands, Highland dancers, and military displays for 10 days (Jul).

Atlantic Seafood Festival, Moncton, New Brunswick: Top chefs prepare some of the world's best seafood (Aug).

Canadian National Exhibition, Toronto: Huge annual exhibition of just about everything (Aug).

Oktoberfest, Kitchener, Ontario: the people of Kitchener invite everyone to sample their Bavarian-style festival of beer, dancing and all things German (Oct).

Christmas Lights Across Canada, Ottawa: Nearly 300,000 lights illuminate the capital to coincide with displays held across the country (Dec).

Train and boat trips

TRAIN
Agawa Canyon (Ontario)
From Sault Ste. Marie, a splendid day trip north through the wilderness of the Canadian Shield with a stop in Agawa Canyon.
☎ 800/242-9287 (toll free); 705/946-7300 (Algoma Central);
www.agawacanyontourtrain.com ⚅ Early Jun to mid-Oct

Polar Bear Express (Ontario)
From Cochrane, a 12-hour return trip north to Moosonee at Arctic tidewater on the shores of James Bay.
☎ 800/265-2356 (toll free); 705/272-5338 (Ontario Northland);
www.ontarionorthland.ca ⚅ Late Jun–late Aug

BOAT
Bonaventure Island
The island is famous for its seabirds. Boats take a circular route around the island and pass close to the Rocher Percé (➤ 46–47).

Alternatively, walk across the island for a closer view of the birds.
☎ 877/782-2974 (toll free); 418/782-2974 🕐 Mid-May to mid-Oct daily 9–5

Maid of the Mist at Niagara Falls (➤ 45)

Thousand Islands (➤ 176)
To experience the area to the fullest, you should take a boat trip.
Some trips stop to visit the amazing six-story extravaganza, Boldt
Castle, on Heart Island, built 1900–1904 by George C. Boldt.
📁 Boat tours to Thousand Islands (expensive) run daily, May–Oct
✉ Gananoque Boat Line: 6 Water Street, Gananoque ☎ 888/717-4837 (toll
free); 613/382-2144; www.ganboatline.com ✉ Rockport Boat Line Ltd:
23 Front Street, Rockport ☎ 800/563-8687 (toll free); 613/659-3402;
www.rockportcruises.com ✉ Kingston 1000 Islands Cruises: 263 Ontario
Street, Kingston ☎ 800/848-1000; 613/549-5544; www.ktic.ca ❓ The castle
is on US soil so passports are required

Western Brook Pond
The only way to properly appreciate this lake is to walk to its
shore and take the two-hour boat trip along its length. The lake is
oligotrophic and has minimal plant life, making its waters pure.
☎ 888/458-2016 (toll free); 709/458-2016; www.bontours.ca 🕐 Jul–Aug
daily 10am, 1pm, 4pm; Jun and Sep 1pm

Whale-watching off Cape Breton
Tours by cabin cruiser or Zodiac inflatable boats (the latter can get
in closer to the whales) depart from Pleasant Bay. Pilot, minke,
humpback and fin are the most likely whales to see.
Cabot Trail Whale Watching ☎ 866/688-2424 (toll free) 🕐 Jul–Oct daily,
11, 1:30, 4 (also 6:30 in Jul)
Captain Mark's Whale and Seal Cruise ☎ 888/754-5112 (toll free);
902/224-1316 🕐 Jun 11:30, 1, 3; Jul–Oct 9:30, 11:30, 1, 3, 5

Whale-watching off Tadoussac (➤ 54–55)

Sports venues

In addition to the sports events listed, each of the stadiums below doubles as a venue for live music and large entertainment events.

HALIFAX, NOVA SCOTIA
Metro Centre
This is the home of the Halifax Mooseheads hockey team, not in the National Hockey League (NHL), but with enthusiastic fans.
✉ Brunswick Street ☎ 902/451-1221; www.halifaxmetrocentre.com

MONCTON, NEW BRUNSWICK
Moncton Coliseum
The Moncton Wildcats hockey team, not in the NHL, play the Mooseheads (see above) and teams from Québec.
✉ 377 Killam Drive ☎ 888/720-5600 (toll free); 506/857-4100; www.monctoncoliseum.com

MONTRÉAL
Bell Centre
They say that hockey is not a sport in Montréal but a religion. The Montréal Canadiens, or "Habs", have a fanatical following.
✉ 1260 rue de la Gauchetière ☎ 514/790-1245; 514/989-2841 (ticket office); www.centrebell.ca 🚇 Bonaventure, Lucien L'Allier

Olympic Stadium
Built for the 1976 Olympic Games, it's now home to the Montréal Expos, one of two Canadian teams playing major league baseball.
✉ 4549 avenue Pierre du Coubertin ☎ 514/252-4141; www.rio.gouv.qc.ca

OTTAWA
Scotiabank Place
Home to the capital's NHL team, the Ottawa Senators and also the Ottawa Rebels who play Canada's official national game: lacrosse.
✉ 1000 Palladium Drive, Kanata ☎ 613/599-0100; www.scotiabankplace.com

TORONTO

Air Canada Centre

Expect big crowds and excitement when Toronto Maple Leafs play hockey at home, especially if they're up against arch-rivals the Montréal Canadiens. The centre also hosts games by the Toronto Raptors NBA team and the Toronto Rock lacrosse team.

🖂 40 Bay Street ☎ 416/815-5500; www.theaircanadacentre.com
🚇 Union Station

BMO Field

Opened in 2007, this is Canada's first stadium constructed specifically for soccer, and can seat 20,000 spectators. It is the home of both Toronto FC and Canada's national soccer team.

🖂 170 Princes' Boulevard, Exhibition Place ☎ 416/263-5700; 416/360-GOAL (ticket office); www.bmofield.com 🚇 Union Station, then 509 streetcar west
🚆 GO train to Exhibition

Rogers Centre

This superb stadium is the home the Toronto Blue Jays, who have won the baseball World Series twice. It also hosts the Argonauts, who play in the Canadian Football League.

🖂 1 Blue Jays Way ☎ 416/341-1707; www.rogerscentre.com 🚇 Union Station, then via Skywalk

Places to take the children

ATLANTIC PROVINCES
CAVENDISH, PRINCE EDWARD ISLAND
Avonlea
The *Anne of Green Gables* books by Lucy Maud Montgomery were set on Prince Edward Island (▶ 100–101). Children can relive the stories, explore the farm and attend an old-fashioned school. Tea room.

✉ 8779 Route 6 ☎ 902/963-3050; www.avonlea.ca ⏰ Mid-Jun to Sep daily 💷 Expensive

ONTARIO
CAMBRIDGE
African Lion Safari
Southwest of Toronto. Home to more than 1,000 African animals – including lions, elephants and monkeys – which roam freely in large game reserves that you can drive through.

✉ Safari Road, Rural Route 1 ☎ 800/461-9453 (toll free); 519/623-2620; www.lionsafari.com ⏰ Late Apr to mid-Oct daily 💷 Expensive

LONDON
Children's Museum
Experience life in the Arctic, dig up dinosaur bones, hunt for cave dwellers, or dress up like an astronaut.

✉ 21 Wharncliffe Road South ☎ 519/434-5726; www.londonchildrensmuseum.ca ⏰ Tue–Sun 10–5 (Fri to 8); also Mon Jun–Aug and public hols 💷 Inexpensive

NIAGARA FALLS
Marineland
Huge aquarium complex with beluga whales, sea lions, walruses and interactive pools with underwater viewing panels. Children can help feed the animals and there are thrill rides.

✉ 7657 Portage Road ☎ 905/356-9565; www.marineland.ca ⏰ Late May to mid-Oct daily 🚌 Niagara People Mover bus (Apr–Dec) 💷 Expensive

OTTAWA
Aboriginal Experiences
Aboriginal Experiences brings aboriginal culture to life with tepees, totem poles, canoes, singing, dancing and storytelling – complete with restaurant serving aboriginal food.

✉ Victoria Island ☎ 877/811-3233 (toll free); 613/564-9494; www.aboriginalexperiences.com 🕐 Late Jun–early Sep daily 💷 Moderate

QUÉBEC
MONTRÉAL
Centre des Sciences de Montréal
Engrossing science center on the waterfront in the Old Port of Montréal. Hands-on exhibits and an IMAX movie theater.

✉ quai King Edward ☎ 877/496-4724 (toll free); 514/496-4724; www.centredessciencesdemontreal.com 🕐 Daily 🚇 Place d'Armes then short walk 💷 Expensive

VAUGHAN
Paramount Canada's Wonderland
This is Canada's premier theme park containing more than 200 attractions for all ages, including North America's best selection of roller coasters, a water park, rides for small children and live shows.

✉ 9580 Jane Street, off Highway 400, Rutherford Road exit ☎ 905/832-8131; www.canadaswonderland.com 🕐 Early May and Sep–early Oct Sat–Sun from 10am; mid-May to end Aug daily from 10am, closing time varies 🚌 Wonderland Express; GO Bus from Yorkdale and York Mills subway stations in Toronto; 165A from Toronto, 4, 20 within York region 💷 Expensive

Great museums

Canada Aviation Museum (▶ 152–153)
The museum, housed in a hangar, is part of the Canada Science and Technology Corporation. This has an excellent collection of vintage aircraft through to contemporary craft.

Canada Science and Technology Museum (▶ 153)
Easily recognized by the lighthouse outside, this large, hands-on museum covers astronomy, space travel, computers and communication as well as many other scientific and technological advances. Largest of its kind in the country.

Canadian Museum of Civilization (▶ 36–37)
A wonderful museum presenting Canada's history in a lively and entertaining way. The building itself is also impressive.

Canadian War Museum (▶ 154)

In 2005, the museum moved to a new location with double the original exhibition space for its interesting displays celebrating Canada's military history.

Maritime Museum of the Atlantic (▶ 88)

This museum presents the fascinating history of seafaring in Halifax. Life-size and model ships and a recreated chandlery are highlights.

Musée d'Archéologie et d'Histoire de Montréal (▶ 117)

This museum devoted to archeology opened in 1992 in a strikingly modern building.

Musée d'Art Contemporain, Montréal (▶ 118)

The only museum in the city that specializes in contemporary art. It's part of the downtown place-des-Arts complex.

Musée des Beaux-Arts de Montréal (▶ 118)

Musée de la Civilisation, Québec City (▶ 128)

Royal Ontario Museum (▶ 164–165)

Canada's largest museum, and still expanding, is certain to have something that will interest all age groups. Among its more than 6 million items is a superb collection of Chinese art.

Science North (▶ 48–49)

Lively with lots of hands-on activities – this will appeal to children and adults alike.

Scenic drives

Acadian Coastal Drive, New Brunswick
Tracing the Atlantic coast from the Nova Scotia border to
Dalhousie, this stunning drive incorporates glorious beaches,
delightful fishing villages, the Kouchibouguac National Park and
the gorgeous Chaleur Bay.

Appalachian Range Route, New Brunswick
Weave your way through this ancient landscape of mountains,
forests, rivers and lakes that extends from the Saint John River
valley to the coast at Chaleur Bay, with the highest peak in the
Maritimes, Mount Carleton, along the way.

Bonne Bay, Newfoundland
Cutting into the Long Range Mountains within Gros Morne
National Park (▶ 95), Bonne Bay stretches deep inland from
the Gulf of St. Lawrence. Route 430, hugging the shore on the
northern side, and Route 431 along the southern side, are
equally scenic.

Cabot Trail, Nova Scotia
Breathtaking views mark this trail which encircles the Cape Breton
Highlands National Park (▶ 38–39) and its forest-cloaked
mountains and rugged coastline.

Fundy Trail, New Brunswick
Experience the highest tides in the world on a route that takes in
the Hopewell Rocks (▶ 96), the Fundy National Park (▶ 94), the
incredible Reversing Falls at Saint John and pretty St. Andrews-by-
the-Sea (▶ 101).

Georgian Bay, Ontario
Beautiful Georgian Bay, dotted with wooded islands, is an offshoot
of Lake Huron. From Wasaga Beach, on Nottawasaga Bay, take
Highway 26 west through Collingwood and Meaford, then loop

round through Annan and Leith to reach Owen Sound, from where you can drive north to the tip of the Bruce Peninsula.

Navigators' Route, Québec
This evocatively named route follows the southern shore of the St. Lawrence River, just east of Québec City, with wonderful views across to the mountains on the north shore. It passes through attractive villages redolent of seafaring heritage.

Niagara Parkway (▶ 173), Ontario
Historic sites, lush vineyards and views of the Niagara River form this route, with the breathtaking Niagara Falls (▶ 44–45) along the way. The Parkway finishes up in the charming little town of Niagara-on-the-Lake (▶ 172) on the shore of Lake Ontario.

North Cape Coastal Drive, Prince Edward Island
From Summerside, this circuit around Prince Edward Island's northwest coast visits fabulous secluded beaches and communities with rich First Nations and Acadian cultures. At low tide, you can walk from North Cape to the longest natural rock reef in North America.

a walk

through the heart of Toronto

Start at City Hall. Cross over Bay Street, then take Albert Street and enter the Eaton Centre (► 79). Exit on Yonge Street and turn right. Turn left at King Street.

To your right is Scotia Plaza, across the street is Commerce Court (Canadian Imperial Bank of Commerce), ahead First Canadian Place and Toronto-Dominion Centre.

Turn left on Bay Street; cross Wellington Street.

To your right on Bay, the triangular gold-sheathed towers house the Royal Bank of Canada.

Mid-block enter Brookfield Place (left).

This elegant galleria, five floors high, incorporates two older buildings and two unusually shaped office towers.

Follow Bay Street past Union Station and under the railroad tracks. Continue under the Gardiner Expressway to the waterfront. Turn right and follow the pathway around York Street slip to Queen's Quay Terminal.

Queen's Quay Terminal houses more than 30 high-end stores, galleries and restaurants.

Follow York Street and the Teamway covered sidewalk back under the expressway and railroad. Cross Front Street and turn right at Wellington Street.

On both sides are the black-glass buildings of the Toronto-Dominion Centre.

Enter the Maritime Life Tower (right), with its wonderful Inuit art. Cross Wellington Street, and walk into the courtyard of the TD Centre.

Life-size bronze cows sit chewing the cud, the work of Saskatchewan sculptor Joe Fafard.

Cross King Street and enter First Canadian Place. Descend by escalator into the PATH, a subterranean network of corridors and walkways. Follow signs back to City Hall.

Distance 4.8km (3 miles)
Time 2–2.5 hours, excluding visits
Start/end point Nathan Phillips Square, in front of Toronto City Hall, Queen Street West
✚ *Toronto 3c*
🚇 Queen, Osgoode
Lunch Pumpernickel's Deli ($$) ✉ Queens Quay Terminal ☎ 416/861-0226

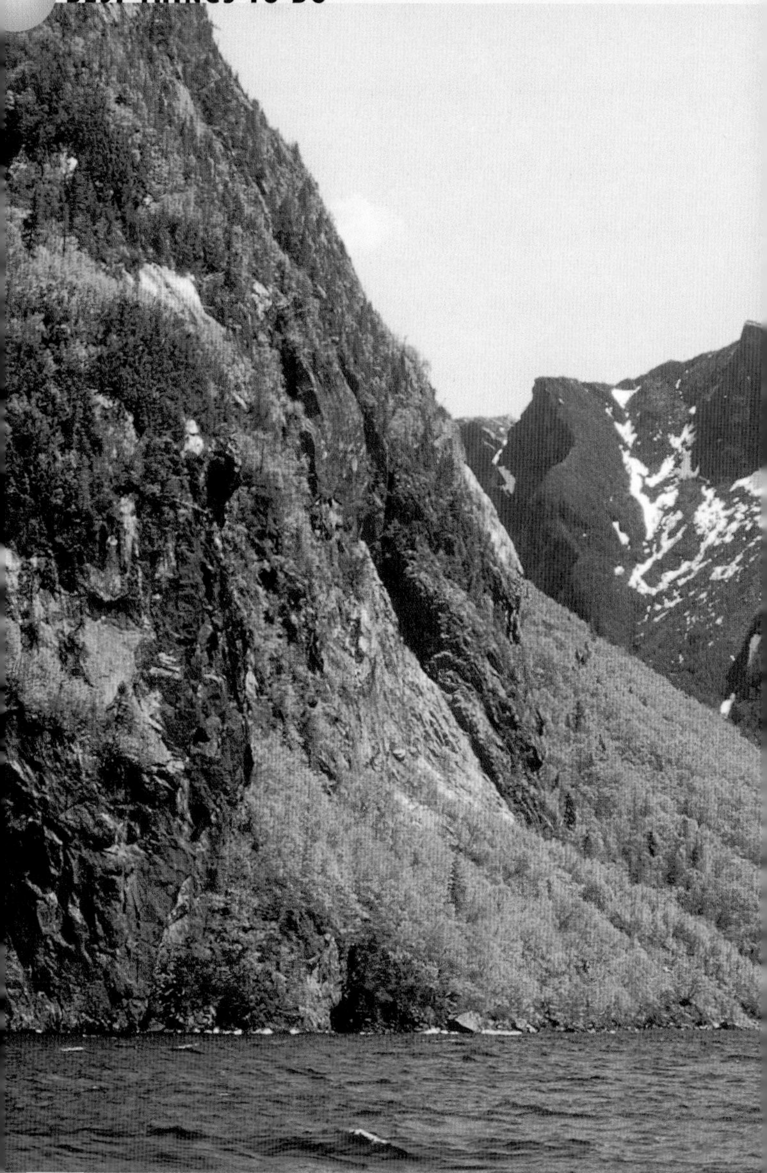

Stunning views

Cape Breton Highlands National Park (➤ 38–39)

Citadel Hill, Halifax (➤ 86)
Views across the harbor and the two bridges across The Narrows.

From the CN Tower (➤ 40–41)

Gros Morne National Park (➤ 95)
Designated a UNESCO World Heritage Site because of its spectacular scenery and geological importance.

Hopewell Rocks, Bay of Fundy (➤ 96)

Niagara Falls (➤ 44–45)

Parc Olympique (➤ 121)
The tower (175m/574ft) that rises over the Olympic Park gives wonderful views – up to 80km (50 miles) in clear weather.

Rocher Percé, Gaspésie (➤ 46–47)

Signal Hill, St. John's (➤ 50–51)

Sunsets over Lake Huron
Lake Huron is a very beautiful stretch of water, a gorgeous deep blue color. Watching the sun set across it on a fine evening is particularly magnificent, as are the occasional summer displays of the aurora borealis in the night sky. The Ontario shoreline both north and south of Goderich has some deserted stretches that are ideal for appreciating these phenomena. The observation tower at Parry Sound has a wonderful view over island-dotted Georgian Bay.

Great restaurants

▼▼▼▼▼ The Cabot Club

Refined restaurant with a great view of Signal Hill
(► 50–51). The traditional Newfoundland dishes
include local seafood and wonderful desserts.

✉ The Fairmont Newfoundland, 115 Cavendish Square,
St. John's ☎ 709/726-4977; www.fairmont.com
🕓 Tue–Sat 6–10pm

▼▼ L'Express

Popular, unpretentious bistro with good seafood,
bouillabaisse, steak tartare and wonderful *frîtes* (fries).
Reservations essential.

✉ 3927 rue St-Denis, Montréal ☎ 514/845-5333 🕓 Mon–Fri
8am–2am, Sat–Sun 10am–1am

▼▼▼▼ North 44

Sophisticated restaurant with creative Continental
cuisine and impeccable service. Duck is a specialty.
Large wine list.

✉ 2537 Yonge Street, Toronto ☎ 416/487-4897;
www.north44restaurant.com 🕓 Mon–Sat 5–11

▼▼▼▼▼ Nuances

Gourmet French cuisine on the top floor of the casino. Great views
over the St. Lawrence River. Business attire.

✉ Pavillon de la France, 5th Floor, Casino du Montréal, 1 avenue du Casino,
Montréal ☎ 514/392-2708; 800/665-2274 ext 2708 (toll free);
www.casino-de-montreal.com 🕓 Daily 5:30–11pm (to 11:30pm Fri and Sat)

▼▼▼▼ Ryan Duffy's Steak and Seafood

This has been on top 100 Canadian restaurants list for more than
25 years. The dishes major on corn-fed steak and local seafood.

✉ 1650 Bedford Row, Halifax ☎ 902/421-1116; www.ryanduffys.ca
🕓 Mon–Fri 11:30–2, 5–10, Sat–Sun 5–10

▼▼▼ Salty's on the Waterfront

The seafood is fresh and includes Atlantic salmon, lobster and mussels. Try to get a harbor view (▶ 84–85). ✉ 1869 Upper Water Street, Halifax ☎ 902/423-6818; www.saltys.ca ⏱ Daily 11:30–10 (check seasonal variations)

▼▼▼▼ Signatures

The restaurant of Ottawa's Cordon Bleu Culinary Arts Institute is one of the highest rated in Canada. Based on traditional classic French cuisine, the food has inspired contemporary touches that make for an exciting menu. ✉ 453 Laurier Avenue East, Ottawa ☎ 888/209-6302 (toll free); 613/236 2460; www.restaurantsignatures.com ⏱ Tue–Sat 5:30–10pm

▼▼▼▼ Truffles

In the Four Seasons Hotel and generally considered to be the best restaurant in town. Contemporary French menu in classy surroundings. Dress code: smart elegant, but jackets not required. ✉ Four Seasons Hotel, 21 Avenue Road, Toronto ☎ 416/964-0411; www.fourseasons.com ⏱ Tue–Sat 6–10

▼▼ Wienstein and Gavino's Pasta Bar

A chic Italian eatery in the middle of the bar and nightclub district with lots of classic Italian main dishes and desserts. ✉ 1434 rue Crescent, Montréal ☎ 514/288-2231; www.wiensteinand gavinos.com ⏱ Daily 11:30–11 (to midnight Thu–Sat), bar open until 3am

Great shopping

Bloor/Yorkville, Toronto

You can sniff affluence on the breeze in this corner of Toronto, where the city's wealthy flit between the designer boutiques and upscale galleries. The neighborhood includes the classy Hazelton Lanes mall. A great place to window shop and people-watch.

✉ Between Yonge, Bloor, Avenue and Davenport, Toronto, Ontario

Byward Market, Ottawa

This is Ottawa's most lively area, with a bustling street market where stands are piled high with fresh food, clothing and gifts. The surrounding streets are lined by specialty stores, boutiques and restaurants. The central market hall is also a venue for events.

✉ Byward Market Square and surrounding streets, Ottawa, Ontario
☎ 613/562-3325; www.byward-market.com ⏰ Daily

Champlain Place, Moncton

The second-biggest shopping mall in the Maritimes and the most central. It has more than 160 stores of all kinds, from the big three

(Sears, Wal-Mart and Sobeys) to fashion, sports and individual specialty stores. The Crystal Palace amusement complex is just across the parking lot.

✉ 477 Paul Street, Dieppe, Moncton, New Brunswick ☎ 506/867-0055; www.champlainplace.ca 🕙 Mon–Sat 10–9, Sun 12–5

Historic Properties, Halifax

In an area that's been a hive of activity for more than 250 years, this heritage district at the historic "Gateway to Canada" is now a great place for browsing (► 86–87).

✉ 1869 Upper Water Street, Halifax, Nova Scotia ☎ 902/429-0530; www.historicproperties.ca 🕙 Daily

Montréal Eaton Centre

Large shopping complex linked into the Underground City, with about 150 fashion stores and other retail outlets.

✉ 705 rue Ste-Catherine Ouest, Montréal, Québec ☎ 514/288-3708; http://centreeaton.shopping.ca 🕙 Mon–Fri 10–9, Sat 10–5, Sun 11–5 🚇 McGill

Quartier Petit Champlain, Québec City

In the historic heart of Québec City, this picturesque district is crammed full of enticing little boutiques selling fashions, crafts, art and jewelry, interspersed with cafés and restaurants.

✉ Lower Town, Québec City, Québec ☎ 418/692-2613; 877/692-2613 (toll free); www.quartierpetitchamplain.com 🕙 Mon–Sat 9:30–9, Sun 9:30–5

Toronto Eaton Centre

Probably Canada's most famous shopping destination, drawing around 50 million visitors a year. It's big, bright and airy and contains more than 250 stores of all kinds and several restaurants.

✉ 220 Yonge Street, between Dundas and Queen streets, Toronto, Ontario ☎ 416/598-8560; www.torontoeatoncentre.com 🕙 Mon–Fri 10–9, Sat 9:30–7, Sun 12–6 🚇 Dundas or Queen

Exploring

Eastern Canada consists of three regions: the Atlantic Provinces, Québec and Ontario. The culture is a blend of Acadian and Qúebecois French, Highland Scots and Irish, while Toronto is one of the most multicultural cities in the world. Here, too, are some historic towns and villages that date back to the earliest settlers, and fishing communities around the coast still land superb seafood.

The scenery in the east of the country matches that elsewhere and there are a number of national parks where you can enjoy the stunning landscape. The major cities are repositories of culture and have some of Canada's best museums.

Atlantic Provinces

At the extreme eastern edge of Canada lie the provinces of New Brunswick, Nova Scotia, Prince Edward Island, and Newfoundland and Labrador. Steeped in the spray of the Atlantic Ocean, they are the smallest of all the Canadian provinces in both size and population.

St John's

Halifax

They are nevertheless strong in their traditional heritage, reflecting French Acadian roots, the earliest Loyalist settlements, the Gaelic culture of the Highland Scots and, in the case of Newfoundland, a strong Irish legacy. They boast major cities such as Halifax, Moncton and St. John's, charming communities like Charlottetown, Fredericton, St. Andrews-by-the-Sea, Lunenburg and Annapolis Royal, and the major historical restorations of Louisbourg and Village Historique Acadien. The scenery is amazingly varied, from the dramatic fjords of Gros Morne and the impressive seascapes of mountainous Cape Breton to the pretty rural landscape of Prince Edward Island and the fabulous tides of the Bay of Fundy.

HALIFAX

Everything in Halifax is marked by the sea. The waterfront is colorful, with a public walkway stretching for miles, while the city's streets are imbued with the ever-present salty feel and smell of the ocean.

Capital of Nova Scotia and the largest city of Atlantic Canada, Halifax is blessed with a magnificent natural harbor that extends nearly 16km (10 miles) inland. The outer harbor is divided from the Bedford Basin by a stretch called The Narrows, where the city climbs up a hill topped by a massive star-shaped fortress. The Citadel continues to dominate the town despite recent highrise construction.

Founded in July 1749, Halifax was from the start a military stronghold and naval base. During World War I, an event occurred that left a terrible mark on the city. In 1917, a French munitions ship, the *Mont Blanc*, had a fatal collision with a Belgian relief ship, the *Imo*, in The Narrows. What followed constituted the greatest man-made explosion the world had seen until the dropping of the atom bomb on Hiroshima in 1945. Not only was a huge area of the city destroyed and a large percentage of the population killed or injured, but even today it's impossible to visit the city without finding some reference to this tragedy.

Today, Halifax remains a naval place, home base for the Canadian Navy's Atlantic fleet, and is also an important commercial

port with huge container terminals. Although the city sometimes suffers from fog and strong winds off the Atlantic, it is a fascinating place to visit - especially when the sun shines.
www.halifaxinfo.com
✚ 21H

Nova Scotia Visitors Centres

ℹ Scotia Square Visitor Centre, 5251 Duke Street, Halifax, Nova Scotia, B3J 1P3 ☎ 902/490-4000
🕐 Daily
ℹ Waterfront Visitor Centre, Sackville Landing, Halifax ☎ 902/490-4000

Art Gallery of Nova Scotia

Located in the heart of the city across the street from the Nova Scotia Legislature, this gallery occupies two 19th-century buildings connected by the Ondaatje Sculpture Court. The collection is made up of mainly Canadian works and the gallery hosts traveling exhibitions. A highlight is part of a house that once belonged to Maud Lewis, an artist from Digby, Nova Scotia, who decorated her home with colorful naive art.

www.artgalleryofnovascotia.ca

✉ 1723 Hollis Street ☎ 902/424-7542 🕐 Daily 10–5 (to 9pm Thu)
✋ Moderate 🍴 Cheapside Café ($) ➤ 58 ❓ Guided tours daily 2:30 (Thu 2:30 and 7pm)

Citadel

Rising above the city, Citadel Hill offers fine views of its harbor and the bridges that span The Narrows to connect Halifax with Dartmouth on the opposite shore. Immediately below you is the Town Clock, a gift to the community from Prince Edward, father of Queen Victoria. The present Citadel, completed in 1865, is a national historic site. As you cross the drawbridge, you will meet staff posing as members of the 78th Highland Regiment, who were stationed here at that time. Wearing MacKenzie tartan kilts they will show you their barracks, guardroom, garrison cell and powder magazine. Each day they fire the noon gun, by which everyone in Halifax sets their clocks.

www.pc.gc.ca/lhn-nhs/ns/halifax

✉ Corner of Sackville and Brunswick streets ☎ 902/426-508 🕘 Early May–Oct 9–5 (to 6pm Jul–Aug); Nov–early May grounds only open ✋ Moderate 🍴 Coffee shop ($) ❓ Regimental gift store. Military drills. Guided tours

Historic Properties

In the 1970s, a number of 19th-century waterfront warehouses were renovated. Known as Historic Properties, they now house craft stores, an excellent food market and several restaurants.

If you walk along the waterfront walkway (4km/2.5 miles) you can visit, among other attractions, the Maritime Museum of the Atlantic (➤ 88), the *Bluenose II* (if she is visiting; ➤ 99) and the ferry to Dartmouth. Beyond the new complexes is Pier 21 which was the entry point to Canada for over a million immigrants between 1928 and 1971, and is now an award-winning musuem.
www.historicproperties.ca

✉ Upper Water Street ☎ 902/429-0530 ♿ Free. Parking: expensive
🍴 Food market and variety of restaurants ($–$$)

Pier 21 National Historic Site
✉ 1055 Marginal Road ☎ 902/425-7770; www.pier21.ca 🕐 May–late Nov daily 9:30–5:30; late Nov–Apr; Tue–Sat 10–5, (also Mon in Apr)
♿ Moderate 🍴 Café ($)

Maritime Museum of the Atlantic

On the waterfront, partly located in the former William Robertson ship's chandlery, this maritime museum boasts a number of full-size ships floating beside it as well as a model collection inside. There are fascinating displays about the *Titanic* (many of the unidentified bodies were buried in Halifax) and the Halifax Explosion (▶ 84). There is also a section devoted to the Cunard Steamship Line, because Samuel Cunard, its founder, was from Halifax. The highlight is probably the restored ship's chandlery of 1879, complete with owner William Robertson behind the counter.

During the summer, you can explore the HMCS *Sackville*, the sole survivor of more than 100 corvettes that were built in Canada to escort convoys across the Atlantic during World War II.

http://museum.gov.ns.ca/mma

✉ 1675 Lower Water Street ☎ 902/424-7490 🕓 May–Oct daily 9:30–5:30 (to 8pm Tue; closed Sun am May and Oct); Nov–Apr Tue 9:30–8, Wed–Sat 9:30–5, Sun 1–5. HMCS *Sackville*: daily, Jun–Sep 💰 Moderate; small additional fee for HMCS *Sackville* 🍴 Restaurants nearby ($–$$)

More to see in the Atlantic Provinces

ANNAPOLIS ROYAL

Twice daily, the great tides of the Bay of Fundy rush into the Annapolis Basin, reversing the flow of the river at tiny Annapolis Royal and providing electricity through North America's only tidal power generating station.

Today, the town is a gracious mixture of heritage and charm, and its main street is lined by elegant homes, craft shops, art galleries and restaurants. Once, however, it was the most fought over place in Canada, changing hands frequently between the English and the French. In tho oontor of the community is **Fort Anne,** whose picturesque site offers sweeping views of the Annapolis Basin from its well-preserved earthworks. A short drive 10.5km (6.5 miles) west takes you to **Port Royal,** founded in 1605 by Samuel de Champlain, making it the first French colony on the continent. The reconstructed wooden buildings form a distinctive compound and contain both working and living areas.

www.annapolisroyal.com

➕ 20G ✉ 236 Prince Albert Road, Box 2, Annapolis Royal, Nova Scotia
☎ 902/532-5454

Fort Anne and Port Royal National Historic Sites

✉ P.O. Box 9, Annapolis Royal, Nova Scotia, B0S 1A0 ☎ 902/532-2397; 902/532-2321 (off season); www.pc.gc.ca/lhn-nhs/ns/fortanne; www.pc.gc.ca/lhn-nhs/ns/portroyal ⊙ Mid-May to mid-Oct daily 9–5:30 (to 6pm Jul–Aug) 🖐 Inexpensive 🍴 Restaurants in Annapolis Royal ($–$$)

AVALON PENINSULA

On the east coast of Newfoundland, the Avalon Peninsula seems to hang suspended from the rest of the island by a narrow isthmus. At longitude 52° 37′ 24″ and latitude 47° 31′ 17″, **Cape Spear** (southeast of St. John's) is the most easterly point of the entire North American continent. Today, it is a national historic park and the lighthouse can be visited. Elsewhere along the peninsula, the coastline is ruggedly beautiful. At St. Vincent's, the deep water allows whales to come close to shore. Bird Rock, off Cape St. Mary's, has colonies of northern gannets, razorbills and murres, while at Witless Bay, huge icebergs can be seen in early summer, along with more whales and seabirds.

✚ 23L ❓ Witless Bay is 31km (19 miles) south of St. John's via Route 10. Cape St. Mary's is 102km (63 miles) south of the Trans-Canada Highway via Route 90. St. Vincent's is 80km (50 miles) south of the Trans-Canada Highway via Route 90.

Cape Spear National Historic Site

✉ P.O. Box 1268, St. John's, Newfoundland and Labrador, A1C 5M9 ☎ 709/772-5367; www.pc.gc.ca/lhn-nhs/nl/spear
🕐 Grounds: daily. Visitor center: mid-May to Labour Day daily 8:30–9, then 10–6 until mid-Oct. Lighthouse: mid-May to mid-Oct daily 10–6
✋ Inexpensive 🍴 Restaurants in St. John's ❓ 11km (7 miles) from St. John's via Route 11

BONAVISTA PENINSULA

On Newfoundland's east coast is the Bonavista Peninsula, which is dotted with a number of picturesque communities. The tiny village of Trinity was once a prosperous fishing center and a lot of its charm remains. Colorful Newfoundland "box" houses are set on a hilly peninsula that has fine views of the ocean and the small protected harbor. Bonavista is another tranquil community, best known for its rocky cape where John Cabot is supposed to have made his first North American landfall.

✚ 23M 🍴 Restaurants in Trinity and Bonavista ($–$$) ❓ Trinity is 74km (46 miles) and Bonavista is 114km (71 miles) from the Trans-Canada Highway at Clarenville via Route 230. Cape Bonavista is 5km (3 miles) from Bonavista

CAMPOBELLO ISLAND

Set at the point where the Atlantic Ocean floods into the Bay of Fundy, Campobello Island has long been famous for its invigorating climate. In the late 19th century, wealthy industrialists built summer homes here, among them the parents of Franklin Delano Roosevelt, U.S. president in 1933–45. Roosevelt and his wife had their own summer "cottage" on the island, which is today the centerpiece of an **international peace park.**

www.campobello.com

✚ 12E 🛈 Campobello Island Visitor Center

☎ 506/752-7043

Roosevelt-Campobello International Park

✉ 459 Route 774, Welshpool ☎ 506/752-2922; www.fdr.net ⏰ Mid-May to mid-Oct daily 10–6

✋ Free

FREDERICTON

New Brunswick's capital is a quiet, pretty city of elm-lined streets set on a wide bend of the St. John River. The excellent **Beaverbrook Art Gallery,** has an outstanding collection of British paintings. About 34km (21 miles) west of the city is **Kings Landing** historical settlement, a fascinating recreation of 19th-century Loyalist life set on a fine site in the St. John valley.

www.city.fredericton.nb.ca

✚ 19H ✉ 11 Carleton Street

☎ 506/460-2041; 888/888-4768 (toll free)

Beaverbrook Art Gallery

✉ 703 Queen Street ☎ 506/458-2028; www.beaverbrookartgallery.org

⏰ Daily 9–5:30 (to 9pm Thu) ✋ Moderate

Kings Landing

✉ 20 Kings Landing Road, Kings Landing; exit 253 of TCH ☎ 506/363-4999; 506/363-4959 (recorded information); www.kingslanding.nb.ca
🕐 Early Jun to mid-Oct daily 10–5
✋ Expensive 🍴 King's Head Inn ($$), café ($), ice-cream parlor

FUNDY ISLANDS

Deer, Grand Manan and Campobello (➤ 92) islands are located in the mouth of Passamaquoddy Bay, geographically closer to Maine, U.S.A. than to Canada. The high tides and currents of the bay act as giant nutrient pumps that lure all kinds of creatures, from herring and tuna to whales. People visit the islands for a quiet retreat, to watch birds and to view whales.

www.grandmanannb.com

www.deerisland.nb.ca

✚ 12E 🛈 Grand Manan Tourist Association and Chamber of Commerce ☎ 506/662-3442; 888/525-1655 (toll free)

🚢 Deer Island ferry daily from L'Etete, New Brunswick (☎ 888/747-7006); Grand Manan ferry daily from Blacks Harbour, New Brunswick (☎ 506/662-3724)

FUNDY NATIONAL PARK

On the Bay of Fundy, this park is a wonderful combination of coastal highlands and shoreline. The bay, with its vast tidal range and cold water, influences the entire park. You can experience this tidal fluctuation on the bay's shores by watching fishing boats come and go. At Alma, it takes less than an hour for the water to go from nothing to waist-deep.

www.pc.gc.ca/pn-np/nb/fundy

✚ 20H ✉ P.O. Box 1001, Alma, New Brunswick, E4H 1B4 ☎ 506/887-6000 🕐 Daily (reception center closed weekends in winter) 🖐 Moderate 🍴 Restaurants, Alma ($–$$)

GROS MORNE NATIONAL PARK

On Newfoundland's west coast is Gros Morne, a spectacularly wild area of fjords, sea coast, forest and mountains. In 1987 it was designated a World Heritage Site by UNESCO for the international importance of its geological features. The Gros Morne Tablelands consist of peridotite from the Earth's mantle. Formed some 450 million years ago, these ocher-colored rocks are an incredibly rare occurrence at the Earth's surface. A visit to the Park Discovery Centre in Woody Point, overlooking beautiful Bonne Bay, offers an excellent introduction.

www.pc.gc.ca/pn-np/nl/grosmorne

✚ 21L ✉ P.O. Box 130, Rocky Harbour, Newfoundland and Labrador, A0K 4N0 ☎ 709/458-2417 ◷ Daily ✋ Moderate 🍴 Food services in Rocky Harbour and Woody Point ($–$$)

HOPEWELL ROCKS

There is nowhere better than this to experience the highest tides in the world. Come at low tide and you can walk on the beach beneath these rocky columns, some rising to more than 16m (52ft) and topped by trees. Return at high tide and they appear as tiny islands in the bay. Check tide tables carefully before descending to the beach – the water rushes in very quickly. An Interpretive Centre (mid-May to mid-Oct daily) explains the phenomenon.

🔒 20H ✉ Located 40km (25 miles south of Moncton on Highway 114)
🕙 Daily (when parking lot is closed, walk from approach road)
✋ Parking: moderate 🍴 Food service ($), picnic area

L'ANSE AUX MEADOWS

Christopher Columbus and John Cabot have gone down in history as the great "discoverers" of North America. This site proves they were beaten to it some 400 years earlier by Vikings. It is thought the Vikings came here seasonally to fish and collect fruit to take back to Scandinavia and for expeditions to mainland Canada. Three buildings have been reconstructed and there's an exhibition and a collection of objects excavated at this UNESCO World Heritage Site.
www.pc.gc.ca/lhn-nhs/meadows

🔒 21M ✉ P.O. Box 70, St. Lunaire-Griquet, Newfoundland and Labrador, A0K 2X0 ☎ 709/623-2608 🕙 Jun–early Oct daily 9–6
✋ Moderate 🍴 Restaurants in St. Anthony, 40km (25 miles away)

LABRADOR

Towering mountains, huge lakes and fast-flowing rivers make Labrador one of the world's few remaining wilderness areas and much of the region is inaccessible. A ferry from St. Barbe on Newfoundland to Blanc Sablon in Québec enables you to access the Labrador coast and drive up it for a short distance, or you can drive Route 389 from Baie Comeau in Québec to Labrador City.

Red Bay (78km/48 miles from the ferry) was the whaling capital of the world in the 16th century. Dozens of Basque fishermen came here to hunt whales in order to supply Europe with oil for lamps and soap. An interpretation center recreates these times.
www.newfoundlandandlabradortourism.com

✚ 18M 🛈 Newfoundland and Labrador Department of Tourism, P.O. Box 8700, St. John's, Newfoundland and Labrador, A1B 4J6 ☎ 709/729-0862; 800/563-6353 (toll free)

Red Bay National Historic Site

✉ P.O. Box 103, Red Bay, Newfoundland and Labrador, A0K 4K0 ☎ 709/920-2142; www.pc.gc.ca/lhn-nhs/nl/redbay 🕐 Early Jun–early Oct daily 9–6
✋ Moderate

LOUISBOURG

At one time, Louisbourg was the great fortress of New France, guarding the St. Lawrence River and the colony. Constructed in the early 18th century, it had the largest garrison in North America. Captured and destroyed by the British in 1758, the fort lay in ruins for two centuries, but today it has risen from the ashes. Covering 4.8ha (12 acres), the site now holds a faithful recreation of a town of the 1740s. From the visitor center you can walk or take a shuttle bus to the entrance. The 50-plus buildings, of wood or roughcast masonry are furnished in 1740s style and populated with suitably attired "residents." Tour the King's Bastion and visit the governor's apartments, and don't miss the barracks, where soldiers will regale you with stories of their everyday lives.

www.pc.gc.ca/lhn-nhs/ns/louisbourg

✚ 22J ✉ 259 Park Service Road, Louisbourg, Nova Scotia, B1C 2L2
☎ 902/733-2280 🕓 Jul–Aug daily 9–5:30; mid-May to Jun and Sep to mid-Oct daily 9:30–5; early May and mid- to late Oct daily 9:30–5, (no animation and limited access to buildings); closed Nov–Apr 👋 Expensive
🍴 Restaurants ($–$$) ❓ Craft demonstrations, military drills, etc

LUNENBURG

Set on a hillside and characterized by narrow streets and wood-framed buildings, Lunenburg radiates the flavor of its seafaring heritage. A UNESCO World Heritage Site since 1995, it has a waterfront active with the fishing and shipbuilding industries that have been the backbone of its prosperity since its foundation in 1753. The bright red buildings of the **Fisheries Museum**

of the Atlantic commemorate this heritage, and offer interesting displays and activities. In summer, the schooner *Bluenose II* is often in the port. Visitors can board the boat for a trip.

www.explorelunenburg.ca

✚ 21G ✉ Blockhouse Road ☎ 902/634-8100

Fisheries Museum of the Atlantic

✉ 68 Bluenose Drive ☎ 902/634-4794; 866/579-4909 (toll free); http://museum.gov.ns.ca/fma 🕓 May–Oct daily 9:30–5:30 (to 7pm Tue–Sat Jul–Aug); Nov–Apr Mon–Fri 9:30–4, but closed holidays 👋 Moderate (Nov to mid-Mar inexpensive) 🍴 Old Fish Factory ($$) (☎ 902/634-3333)

PRINCE EDWARD ISLAND

Tiny Prince Edward Island (known as PEI) has quiet rural landscapes, bright red soil and fine sandy beaches and is connected to the mainland by Confederation Bridge. PEI is known worldwide as the setting for Lucy Maud Montgomery's classic tale of redheaded orphan, *Anne of Green Gables* and fans of the book shouldn't miss visiting period-furnished **Green Gables House.**

The island's capital, Charlottetown, is a delightful place to saunter around. It was the birthplace of Canada, following a meeting of colonial movers and shakers who came to discuss confederation in 1864 in the stately Province House. **Founders Hall,** with costumed guides, traces the country's history.

www.gov.pe.ca

🚩 20H ✉ Box 940, Charlottetown, Prince Edward Island, C1A 7M5

☎ 902/368-4444; 800/463-4734 (toll free)

Charlottetown Visitor Centre ✉ 6 Prince Street ☎ 902 368-6613; 800/463-4PEI (toll-free)

Green Gables House ✉ Route 6, Cavendish, Prince Edward Island National Park ☎ 902/963-7874; www.pc.gc.ca/lhn-nhs/pe/greengables ◷ Jul–late Aug daily 9–6 (to 8pm Tue and Thu); May–Jun and late Aug–Oct daily 9–5; Apr and Nov–late Dec Sun–Thu 10–4; early Jan–Mar Sun–Thu noon–4. Closed Easter ✋ Moderate 🍽 Café ($)

Founders Hall ✉ 6 Prince Street, Charlottetown ☎ 902/368-1864; 800/955-1864 (toll free); www.foundershall.ca ◷ Mid-May to early Oct daily; early Oct–Nov and Feb to mid-May Tue–Sat. Closed Dec–Jan ✋ Moderate

ST. ANDREWS-BY-THE-SEA

Right at the end of a peninsula extending into Passamaquoddy Bay, St. Andrews-by-the-Sea is a small community and a National Historic District. It was settled by Loyalists in 1783, and its tree-lined streets are named after King George III's 15 children. Later, St. Andrews became a fashionable place for the wealthy to build summer homes.

The town has many attractions, including the **Huntsman Marine Science Centre** but find time to stroll the quaint streets and admire the Georgian houses as well.

www.townofstandrews.ca; **www.**townsearch.com/standrews
🚆 12E 🛈 St. Andrews Chamber of Commerce: 46 Reed Avenue, St. Andrews-by-the-Sea, New Brunswick, E5B 1A1 ☎ 506/529-3555; 800/563-7397 (toll free)

Huntsman Marine Science Centre

✉ 1 Lower Campus Road ☎ 506/529-1200; www.huntsmanmarine.ca ◷ Late May–early Sep daily 10–5; early Sep–late May Thu–Sun 10–5 (seal feeding times 11am and 4pm) ✋ Moderate

ST. JOHN'S

Facing the open Atlantic in the extreme east of Newfoundland, the province's capital has a spectacular site on the slopes of a natural harbor. The steep streets are a clutter of colorful wooden houses and the harbor is full of the ships

of many nations. St. John's inhabitants, many of Irish descent, have a distinctive accent and a great sense of humor; and they adore their city.

One downtown landmark that's hard to miss is **The Rooms,** a brightly painted structure resembling a giant group of the old fish processing "rooms". It's Newfoundland's premier cultural center, containing the provincial museum, art gallery and archives, artists in residence, a multimedia theater and performance space.

From the harbor, there are boat trips to view whales and the summer icebergs. Peek inside the Murray Premises Hotel, renovated 1846 fishing warehouses (➤ 106), and on the road to Signal Hill (➤ 50–51) note the entrance to the **Johnson Geo Centre,** a great geological showcase constructed underground.

www.stjohns.ca

✚ 23L ⬛ City Hall 1st Floor, 35 New Gower Street, St. John's, Newfoundland and Labrador, A1C 5M2 ☎ 709/576-8106

The Rooms

✉ 9 Bonaventure Avenue ☎ 709/757 8000; www.therooms.ca 🕐 Jun to mid-Oct Mon–Sat 10–5 (to 9pm Wed), Sun noon–5; mid-Oct to May Tue–Sat 10–5 (to 9pm Wed and Thu), Sun noon–5 💵 Moderate (free Wed 6–9pm)

Johnson Geo Centre

✉ 175 Signal Hill Road ☎ 709/737-7880; 866/868-7625 (toll free); www.geocentre.ca 🕐 Mon–Sat 9:30–5, Sun noon–5; closed Mon mid-Oct to mid-May 💵 Moderate ❓ Geo-boutique with geological items

TERRA NOVA NATIONAL PARK

At Terra Nova, on the east coast of Newfoundland, forested hills rise above a rocky, fjord-like coastline, creating an area rich in wildlife and scenic beauty. Moose, lynx and black bear haunt the forests, bald eagles and great horned owls soar overhead, and whales and other marine life frequent the waters offshore.

Terra Nova is easily accessible, since the Trans-Canada Highway

bisects it. Most park facilities are located on Newman Sound, including the Marine Interpretation Centre in Saltons. There are also boat tours, which provide opportunities for observing different aspects of the life of the Sound, and several viewpoints on land.

www.pc.gc.ca/pn-np/nl/terranova

✚ 23M ✉ Glovertown, Newfoundland and Labrador, A0G 2L0. 240km (149 miles) from St. John's ☎ 709/533-28001 🕐 Daily (visitor center closed Tue–Wed early Jan–late Apr) 👣 Moderate 🚤 For boat tours on Newman Sound, contact Ocean Watch Tours (☎ 709/533-6024)

VILLAGE HISTORIQUE ACADIEN

Located on New Brunswick's Acadian Peninsula, this recreated village provides an authentic representation of French Acadian life between 1770 and 1939. The story of the Acadians is a sad one. Expelled from their farmlands in Nova Scotia in 1755, most of these settlers were deported to the southern British colonies. Eventually some made their way north again to settle in this area.

Interpreters in period costume bring the place to life, and visitors can explore the 40 buildings and watch displays to discover more about Acadian customs and trades.

www.villagehistoriqueacadien.com

✚ 19J ✉ 14311 Road 11, P.O. Box 5626, Caraquet, New Brunswick, E1W 1B7. 10km (6 miles) west of Caraquet in northeastern New Brunswick ☎ 506/726-2600; 877/721-2200 (toll free) ⏰ Early Jun to mid-Sep daily 10–6; mid-Sep to late Sep daily 10–5 (5 buildings open) ✋ Expensive ⭐ Restaurant and food services ($–$$) ❓ Store selling Acadian items

HOTELS

CHARLOTTETOWN, PRINCE EDWARD ISLAND
▽▽▽▽ The Great George ($$$)

This inn has several properties, providing luxury accommodations in 19th-century style. Some rooms have fireplace and Jacuzzi, and all are elegantly furnished with antiques. Breakfast included.

✉ 58 Great George Street ☎ 902/892-0606; 800/361-1118 (toll free); www.thegreatgeorge.com

CHÉTICAMP
▽▽ Cabot Trail Sea and Golf Chalets ($$)

Just outside the Cape Breton Highlands National Park, this complex offers one- or two-bedroom housekeeping chalets. A private path leads to the golf course.

✉ 71 Fraser Doucet Lane, PO Box 324 ☎ 902/224-1777; 877/244-1777 (toll free); www.seagolfchalets.com

FREDERICTON, NEW BRUNSWICK
▽▽▽▽ Crowne Plaza Fredericton Lord Beaverbrook Hotel ($$$)

Elegant hotel with unbeatable location downtown near the Legislative Assembly and Beaverbrook Art Gallery (➤ 92). The Terrace restaurant overlooks the St. John River.

✉ 659 Queen Street ☎ 506/455-3371; 877/579-7666 (toll free); www.cpfredericton.com

HALIFAX
▽▽▽▽ Waverley Inn ($$)

Historic bed-and-breakfast, with hardwood floors and fine antique furniture, in a peaceful area close to downtown.

✉ 1266 Barrington Street ☎ 902/423-9346; 800/565-9346; www.waverleyinn.com

NORTH RUSTICO, PRINCE EDWARD ISLAND
▽▽ Gulf View Cottages ($$)

Fully equipped two-bedroom cottages with a fine site overlooking the Gulf of St. Lawrence in Prince Edward Island National Park. Cycling and jogging trails; beach.

✉ Gulf Shore Road ☎ 902/963-2052; 877/963-2052 (toll free);
www.gulfviewcottages.com ⏱ Closed early-Oct to late-May

ST. JOHN'S, NEWFOUNDLAND
〰〰〰 Murray Premises Hotel ($$$)
Former warehouse overlooking the harbor, restored as a luxurious
boutique hotel. Old beams and exposed brickwork beautifully set
off the up-to-the-minute facilities. Two restaurants.
✉ 5 Becks Cove ☎ 709/738-7773; 866/738-7773 (toll free);
www.murraypremiseshotel.com

RESTAURANTS

ANNAPOLIS ROYAL, NOVA SCOTIA
〰〰〰 Garrison House Dining Room ($$)
In a 19th-century house opposite Fort Anne (➤ 89). Good food in
small intimate dining rooms. Seafood specialties.
✉ 350 St. George Street ☎ 902/532-5750; 866/532-5750; www.garrison
house.ca ⏱ Early May to mid-Dec daily 5–8 (to 9pm high season)

CHARLOTTETOWN, PRINCE EDWARD ISLAND
〰〰 Chez Cora ($–$$)
This Québec-based breakfast-and-lunch chain is going from
strength to strength. They serve a terrific range of good healthy
food (fresh fruit with everything) and deliciously naughty treats.
✉ 476 Queen Street ☎ 506/472-2672; www.chezcora.com

〰〰 Gahan House ($–$$)
Traditional brew-pub with above-average food, including fish and
chips coated in batter made with the brewery's own ale.
✉ 126 Sydney Street ☎ 902/626-2337; www.gahan.ca ⏱ Mon–Thu 11–11,
Fri–Sat 11am–1am, Sun 11–9 (kitchen closes one hour before closing time)

DIEPPE, NEW BRUNSWICK
〰〰〰 L'Idylle ($$–$$$)
An elegant restaurant in an 1828 home, where owner/chef Emm-
anuel Charretier and his wife, both from France, serve authentic
French cuisine (and grow many of the vegetables and fruits).

✉ 1788 Amirault Street ☎ 506/860-6641; www.restaurantidylle.com
🕐 Mon–Sat 5–10pm

FREDERICTON, NEW BRUNSWICK
〰〰 Brewbakers ($$)
Seafood, crispy pizza from the wood-fired oven and interesting salads are served in a warren of rooms as well as on an outdoor patio and in the bar.
✉ 546 King Street ☎ 506/459-0067; www.brewbakers.ca 🕐 Mon–Thu 11:30–10, Fri 11:30–11, Sat 4–11, Sun 4–10

SAINT JOHN, NEW BRUNSWICK
〰〰 Steamers Lobster Company ($$–$$$)
There's lobster, of course, in this restaurant specializing in market-fresh local seafood. There are also meat choices such as prime rib and stir fries. Dinner theater some nights.
✉ 110 Water Street ☎ 506/648-2325; www.steamerslobstercompany.com
🕐 Daily 4–10

HALIFAX, NOVA SCOTIA
〰〰〰 McKelvie's Delishes Fishes Dishes ($–$$)
In a refurbished firehouse with an outdoor patio in the summer months. A great place for seafood, pasta, chowders, and desserts.
✉ 1680 Lower Water Street ☎ 902/421-6161; www.mckelvies.com
🕐 Mon–Sat 11:30–10, Sun 4:30–10

〰〰〰 Salty's on the Waterfront ($$–$$$)
See page 77.

MOBILE, NEWFOUNDLAND
〰〰 Captain's Table ($$)
Named after Captain William Jackman, a Newfoundland hero. Great seafood, chowder and other traditional Newfoundland dishes. Pleasant dining room with open fireplace.
✉ Mobile ☎ 709/334-2278; www.captainstable.nf.ca 🕐 Daily 11:30–9; Oct 1–Apr 30 Wed–Sun noon–8

ST. JOHN'S, NEWFOUNDLAND
▼▼▼ The Cellar ($$–$$$)
Fine dining with some local dishes and an extensive wine list.

✉ 189 Water Street ☎ 709/579-8900; www.thecellarrestaurant.ca

🕓 Mon–Fri 11:30–2:30, 5:30–9:30 (10pm Fri), Sat 5:30–10, Sun 5:30–9:30

SUMMERSIDE, PRINCE EDWARD ISLAND
▼▼ Starlite Diner ($)
A 1950s-style diner, complete with jukeboxes in the booths.
Home-style cooking, including fried clams, burgers, barbecued
chicken, hot dogs and great desserts.

✉ 810 Water Street ☎ 902/436-7752; www.starlitediner.pe.ca

SHOPPING

SHOPPING CENTERS AND MALLS
Avalon Mall
Northwest of the city. Attractive mall on two levels, with 140
stores, including clothing, books, music, gifts and jewelry stores,
Sobeys supermarket and Wal-Mart. Large movie theater complex;
food court and restaurants.

✉ 48 Kenmount Road, St. John's, Newfoundland ☎ 709/753-7144;
www.shopavalonmall.com 🕓 Mon–Sat 10–10, Sun 12–5

Champlain Place
See pages 78–79.

Halifax Shopping Centre
To the west of downtown. Biggest mall in the Maritimes, with
over 170 stores, including boutiques, sports stores, pharmacies,
banks, Sears and Wal-Mart. Fast-food outlets.

✉ 7001 Mumford Road, Halifax, Nova Scotia ☎ 902/453-1752;
www.halifaxshoppingcentre.com 🕓 Mon–Sat 9:30–9; Sun noon–5

MARKETS
Boyce Farmers' Market
About 200 vendors sell local produce, crafts and gifts at this
longtime institution in downtown.

✉ 665 George Street, Fredericton, New Brunswick ☎ 506/451-1815; www.boycefarmersmarket.com ⏰ Sat 6am–1pm

Halifax Farmers' Market
In the courtyards of a former brewery, this market is a hive of activity on Saturdays. Relocating to a spectacular new location on the waterfront, when it will operate six days a week.

✉ Keith's Brewery Building, 1496 Lower Water Street (moving to Pier 20), Halifax, Nova Scotia ☎ 902/492-4043; http://halifaxfarmersmarket.com ⏰ Sat 7am–1pm

CRAFTS, ANTIQUES AND OTHER SPECIALTIES
Great Village Antiques Marketplace
This is Nova Scotia's biggest antiques market, with 18 specialist dealers. China, glass, furniture, folk art, toys, jewelry, and more.

✉ 8728 Highway 2, Great Village (northwest of Truro, off Trans-Canada Highway), Nova Scotia ☎ 902/668-2149; www.greatvillageantiques.com ⏰ Mar–Dec Mon–Sat 10–5, Sun 1–5

River Valley Crafts and Artisan Gift Shops
A number of craftspeople sell their wares such as painting, jewelry, First Nations crafts and Celtic art on the main floor of the former Soldiers' Barracks in downtown's historic Garrison district.

✉ Barracks Square, Carleton Street, Fredericton, New Brunswick ☎ 506/460-2837; 888/888-4768 ⏰ Closed Oct–May

ENTERTAINMENT

CHILDREN'S ENTERTAINMENT
Fluvarium
Windows below water level show the life of a real stream full of trout, frogs and tadpoles. Feeding time 4pm.

✉ Nagles Place, Pippy Park, St. John's, Newfoundland ☎ 709/754-3474; www.fluvarium.ca ⏰ Mon–Fri 9–5, Sat–Sun 12–5 ✋ Inexpensive

Science East
More than 100 exhibits. Children can step inside a huge kaleido-scope or see their hair stand on end in the static electricity display.

✉ 668 Brunswick Street, Fredericton, New Brunswick ☎ 506/457-2340; www.scienceeast.nb.ca 🕐 Jun–Aug Mon–Sat 10–5, Sun 1–4; Sep–May Mon–Fri 12–5, Sat 10–5 💲 Inexpensive

THEATERS AND NIGHTCLUBS
Grafton Street Dinner Theatre
Specializes in lighthearted musical comedies served up during dinner by staff in costume. Audience participation encouraged.
✉ 1741 Grafton Street, Halifax, Nova Scotia ☎ 902/425-1961; www.graftonstdinnertheatre.com

King's Theatre
Live theater, concerts and movies presented year-round in a historic building on the town's main street. Also a summer festival.
✉ 209 St. George Street, Annapolis Royal, Nova Scotia ☎ 902/532-7704; 902/532-5466 (24-hour listings); www.kingstheatre.ca

Neptune
Famous Canadian theater company presenting drama, music and comedy in two auditoriums year-round.
✉ 1593 Argyle Street, Halifax, Nova Scotia ☎ 902/429-7070; 800/565-7345 (toll free); www.neptunetheatre.com

Olde Dublin Pub
Irish pub open year-round, with live entertainment and traditional music on Saturdays and Sundays, May–September.
✉ 131 Sydney Street, Charlottetown, Prince Edward Island
☎ 902/892-6992; www.oldedublinpub.com

The Playhouse
Next to the Provincial Legislature. Theater presenting drama, comedy and all kinds of musical performances year-round.
✉ 686 Queen Street, Fredericton, New Brunswick ☎ 506/458-8344; 866/884-5800 (toll free); www.theplayhouse.nb.ca

Québec

The heart of French Canada, the province of Québec is simply gigantic, extending 1,900km (1,200 miles) north from the U.S. border to the shores of the Hudson Strait. A land of sharp contrasts, it is resolutely distinct in its culture and lifestyle.

Traversed by the magnificent St. Lawrence, one of the world's

great rivers, Québec boasts some spectacular scenery. The Gaspé Peninsula has awe-inspiring seascapes, Saguenay Fjord is bounded by impressive cliffs and filled with dark waters, and the Charlevoix coast offers sweeping views of river and hinterland. Elsewhere, visitors can enjoy the tranquility of the Eastern Townships or the bustling sports-oriented ambience of the Laurentians. Add to these cosmopolitan, sophisticated Montréal, with its great restaurants and summer festivals, and the old-world charm of the capital, Québec City, and the great diversity of the province can be fully appreciated.

MONTRÉAL

Montréal is urbane, sophisticated and cosmopolitan. Although this is the second-largest French-speaking city in the world, fully one-third of the population is non-French, giving it a tremendous cultural vitality.

In 1642, Ville-Marie de Montréal was founded as a Roman Catholic mission; even a hundred years ago it was dominated by the towers and spires of its churches, gaining it the moniker "the city of one hundred steeples." This religious heritage is still evident in the city's churches, even though they stand empty today. It is also evident in the cross on top of Mont-Royal, illuminated at night.

In 1760, the British conquered the city and the economy became the domain of a group of industrious Scots. They expanded the fur trade, founded banks, built the railroads and left their mark on the city architecturally in the form of stone and brick buildings. The late 20th century saw the "reconquest" of the city by the Québécois, and its face is now resolutely French.

Today, Montréal's economy is vibrant, with a strong high-tech orientation and a major port despite its location a thousand miles from the open ocean. The downtown area is flourishing, with the construction of some magnificent buildings, all interconnected by the passageways and plazas of the Underground City, born of Montréal's long, cold winter, which has an average snowfall of 3m (nearly 10ft), more than any other major city on Earth.

www.tourisme-montreal.org

✚ 9D

Centre Infotouriste

✉ 1255 rue Peel, Suite 100, Montréal, Québec, H3B 1N1 ☎ 514/873-2015; 877/266-5687 (toll free) 🕐 Jun–early Sep daily 7am–8pm; May and early Sep–Oct daily 7:30–6; Nov–Apr daily 9–6 🚇 Peel

🛈 174 rue Notre-Dame Est ☎ 514/873-2015; 877/266-5687 (toll free) 🕐 Daily 9–5 (to 7pm late Jun–early Oct)

Basilique Notre-Dame de Montréal (Notre-Dame Basilica)

Built in 1923–29 the twin towers of Montréal's most famous Catholic church rise up over 69m (226ft) on the south side of place d'Armes.

The extraordinary interior of the church was the masterpiece of Victor Bourgeau, a local architect. It is handcarved in wood, mainly red pine, and decorated with 22-carat gold. Above the main altar, the reredos features scenes of sacrifice from the Bible sculpted in white pine. Don't miss the Chapelle du Sacre Coeur (Sacred Heart Chapel), rebuilt in 1982 after a fire, which is dominated by a 15m-high (50ft) bronze depicting humanity's journey through life towards heaven, the work of Charles Daudelin.

www.basiliquenddm.org

➕ *Montréal 6c* ✉ 110 rue Notre-Dame Ouest ☎ 514/842-2925; 866/842-2925 (toll free) 🕐 Daily ✋ Moderate (no charge for attending Mass)

🍴 Restaurants nearby ($–$$$) 🚇 Place d'Armes ❓ Guided tours

Biodôme

Within the former Olympic cycling stadium, four climate-controlled ecosystems have been created with real plantlife and animals. The areas represent a tropical forest, the Laurentian Forest, the underwater world of the St. Lawrence River, and polar regions. The many highlights include the penguins in the Polar World and taking refuge in the "tropics" on a winter's day.

www.biodome.qc.ca

➕ *Montréal 2f (off map)* ✉ 4777 avenue Pierre-de-Coubertin ☎ 514/868-3000 🕐 Daily 9–5 (to 6pm in summer). Closed Mon mid-Sep to Feb ✋ Expensive 🍴 Restaurants and cafés on site ($–$$) 🚇 Viau

Cathédrale Anglicane de Christ Church
(Christ Church Cathedral)

Squeezed in between towering office blocks and a shopping center, this Anglican cathedral (built between 1856 and 1859) is a fine example of neo-Gothic architecture. It has a flamboyant triple portico on rue Ste-Catherine decorated with gables, gargoyles and grotesques, and a courtyard cloister at the back. Inside, walk up the nave below Gothic arches into the chancel, which has a copy of Leonardo da Vinci's *Last Supper*. Just above the pulpit, note the cross created from nails collected in the ruins of England's Coventry Cathedral after it was bombed in 1940.

www.montreal.anglican.org/cathedral

✠ *Montréal 2c* ✉ 635 rue Ste-Catherine Ouest ☎ 514/843-6577 ◷ Daily
✋ Free 🍴 Restaurant in shopping mall beneath cathedral ($) Ⓜ McGill
❓ Lunchtime concerts

Chapelle Notre-Dame-de-Bonsecours
(Chapel of Notre-Dame-de-Bonsecours)

This waterfront church was adopted by 19th-century sailors as their special church and a large statue of the Virgin with arms outstretched faces the river outside. Within the church, don't miss the grisaille frescoes, painted onto the wooden vault by François-Édouard Meloche in 1886. They recount scenes in the life of the Virgin and are executed in a *trompe l'oeil* style. The adjoining museum is devoted to Marguerite Bourgeoys, who settled in Montréal in 1653, built the original chapel on this site, and was canonized in 1982. There is a magnificent view from the tower.

www.marguerite-bourgeoys.com

✠ *Montréal 8f* ✉ 400 rue St-Paul Est ☎ 514/282-8670 ◷ May–Oct
Tue–Sun 10–5:30; Nov to mid-Jan and Mar–Apr Tue–Sun 11–3:30; closed
mid-Jan to Feb ✋ Free. Museum: moderate 🍴 Restaurants nearby ($–$$$)
Ⓜ Champ-de-Mars ❓ Summer theatrical presentations; winter concerts

Jardin Botanique de Montréal (Montréal Botanical Gardens)

These splendid gardens extend over 73ha (180 acres). They consist of nearly 30 thematic gardens and 10 greenhouses with more than 22,000 different species from around the world. The Chinese Garden includes a number of pagodas set around a lake. The First Nations Garden has winding paths, trees and a lake populated with wildfowl. In summer, the gardens of annuals and perennials, and the rose garden, are glorious. The conservatories feature magnificent orchids, tropical plants, ferns and bonsai.

www.ville.montreal.qc.ca/jardin

🚩 *Montréal 2f (off map)* ✉ 4101 rue Sherbrooke Est ☎ 514/872-1400
🕐 Daily 9–5 (to 6pm mid-May to early Sep; 9pm early Sep–Oct). Closed Mon early Jan to mid-May ✋ Expensive May–Oct; moderate rest of year. Parking charge 🍴 Cafeteria ($) 🚇 Pie IX, Viau ❓ Guided tours; balade (small train) tour (free). Horticultural gift store

L'Oratoire St-Joseph (St. Joseph's Oratory)

Set on the north slope of Mont-Royal is the Roman Catholic
shrine of L'Oratoire St-Joseph, whose huge dome is visible from
all over the city. Founded in 1904, it is visited by millions every
year and recent improvements to the site have enhanced access
and facilities.

✚ *Montréal 1e (off map)* ✉ 3800 Chemin Queen-Mary ☎ 514/733-8211;
877/672-8647 (toll free); www.saint-joseph.org ④ Daily 🍴 Cafeteria ($)
Ⓜ Côte-des-Neiges ❓ Religious gift store

Mont-Royal

Best places to see, ➤ 42–43.

Musée d'Archéologie et d'Histoire de Montréal
(Pointe-à-Callière Museum of Archeology and History)

Set on the point of land in Old Montréal where the city started life
in 1642, this is an intriguing museum in a striking modern building.
A short multimedia presentation provides an introduction to the
history of the site. Then you can proceed down to an archeological
crypt to inspect remains of the old city walls and buildings with

English- or French-speaking laser
holograms acting as residents. Climb the
stairs into the old Customs House for
more exhibitions, or take the elevator up
the tower for great views over the river.

www.pacmuseum.qc.ca

✚ *Montréal 7c* ✉ 350 place Royale
☎ 514/872-9150 ④ Late Jun–Aug Mon–Fri
10–6, Sat–Sun 11–6; Sep–late Jun Tue–Fri 10–5,
Sat–Sun 11–5 ✋ Expensive 🍴 Restaurant
l'Arrivage ($$) Ⓜ Place d'Armes ❓ Boutique
with gifts and books at 150 rue St-Paul, Tue–Sun
11–6 (also Mon in summer)

Musée d'Art Contemporain (Museum of Contemporary Art)

Montréal's contemporary art museum is part of the performing arts complex at Place des Arts (➤ 148), which also includes theaters and a concert hall. The museum building is recognizable by the pair of giant lips on its roof, called La Voie lactée (The Milky Way), an artwork by Geneviève Cadieux. This was the first museum in Canada devoted solely to contemporary art, and its approach remains innovative.

www.macm.org

✚ Montréal 3e ✉ 185 rue Ste-Catherine Ouest ☎ 514/847-622
🕐 Tue–Sun 11–6 (to 9pm Wed); also Mon late Jun–early Sep 💵 Moderate (free Wed 6–9pm) 🍴 Restaurant La Rotonde ($$$), café ($) 🚇 Place-des-Arts
🚌 15, 55, 80, 129, 535 ❓ Art bookstore and gift store

Musée des Beaux-Arts de Montréal (Montréal Museum of Fine Arts)

Featuring an encyclopedic collection of art dating from antiquity to contemporary times the musuem is spilt over two sites. On the north side of Sherbrooke Street, a Beaux-Arts building of 1912, houses the Canadian Collection, including some splendid Inuit works. Across the street is Moshe Safdie's 1991 pavilion, which hosts the galleries of European and contemporary art, as well as temporary exhibitions. Connecting the two are vast underground vaults lined with works of ancient civilizations (China, Japan and the Middle East), and African and pre-Columbian art.

www.mmfa.qc.ca

✚ Montréal 1d (off map) ✉ 1379 and 1380 rue Sherbrooke Ouest
☎ 514/285-2000; 800/899-6873 (toll free) 🕐 Tue 11–5, Wed–Fri 11–9, Sat–Sun 10–5 💵 Permanent collection: free. Temporary exhibits: expensive
🍴 Restaurant ($$$), cafeteria ($) 🚇 Guy-Concordia 🚌 Bus 24

Parc Jean-Drapeau (Jean-Drapeau Park)

This park is composed of two islands and has a superb location in the middle of the St. Lawrence River that offers unparalleled views of the city. Together, Île Ste-Hélène and Île Notre-Dame provided the site for the 1967 World's Fair (Expo 67). Two of the former pavilions remain; one houses the Montréal Casino; the other, the Biosphère, an environmental museum. La Ronde amusement park (➤ 147) and the Stewart Museum are also located here.

www.parcjeandrapeau.com

🛉 *Montréal 8f (off map)* ✉ 1 circuit Gilles-Villeneuve ☎ 514/872-6120
🕐 Daily 6am–midnight 🚇 Jean-Drapeau 🚌 Bus 169 access to islands, 167 on islands ⛴ Ferry from Jacques Cartier Pier, Vieux-Port late Jun–early Sep

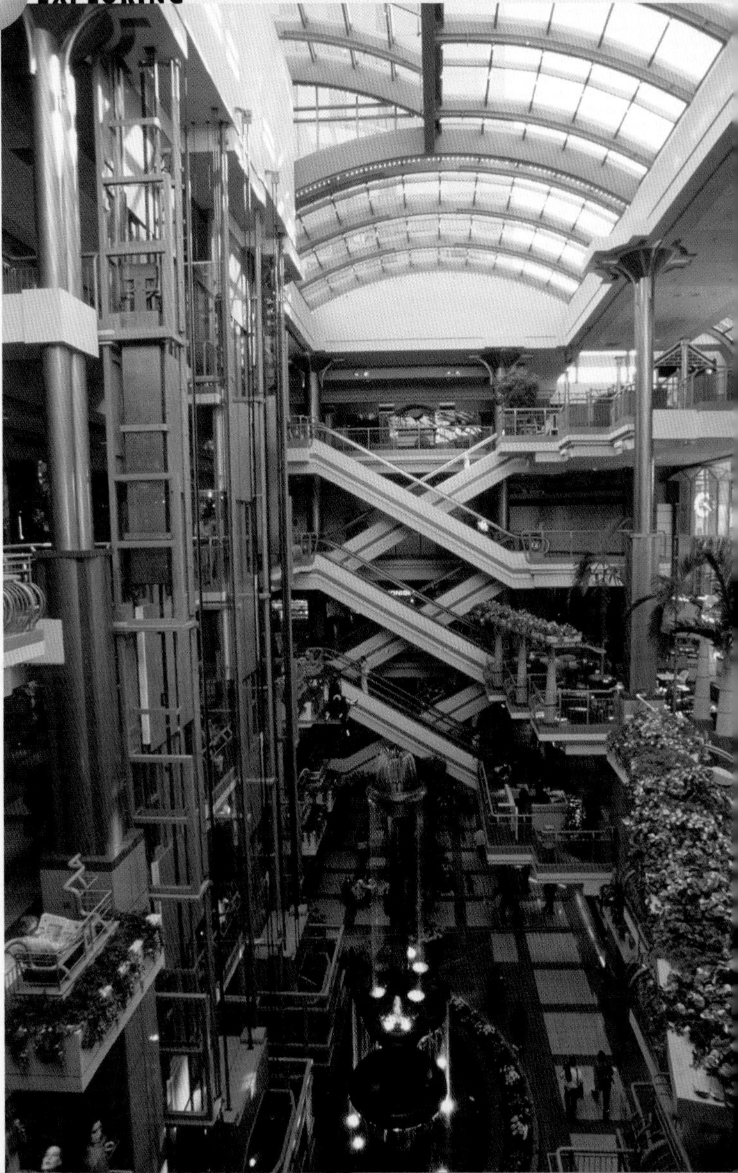

Parc Olympique (Olympic Park)

Site of the summer Olympic games of 1976, Olympic Park is dominated by a huge elliptical stadium that sports a leaning tower and strange roof. Controversial because of its cost, it is nonetheless a remarkable building and the view of the city from the top of the tower is spectacular. It rises to 175m (574ft) at an angle of 45 degrees, and ascent is via an external funicular that offers an exhilarating ride. Beside the stadium stands the Biodôme, which was used for the cycling events of the Olympic games (➤ 114).

www.rio.gouv.qc.ca

🚣 *Montréal 2f (off map)* ✉ 4141 avenue Pierre-de-Coubertin ☎ 514/252-4141 🕐 Daily 9–5 (to 7pm mid-Jun to early Sep) ✋ Guided tours: moderate. Ascent of tower: expensive 🍴 Café 🚇 Pie IX, Viau ❓ Ball games and other sports events; trade shows

Underground City (Reseau Pietonnier Souterraine)

Montréalers have learned to cope with their harsh winters by developing a weatherproof system in downtown that gives priority to pedestrians. This network of passageways, atriums and wide open spaces, extends for more than 33km (20 miles) and connects more than 60 buildings, 40 entertainment venues and eight métro stations, is known as the Underground City, although not all of it is strictly underground. It all started with place Ville-Marie, the huge cruciform tower designed by I.M.Pei in 1962. Highlights include Le Complexe Les Ailes; Promenades Cathèdrale, an architecturally impressive complex below Christ Church Cathedral (➤ 115); Cours Mont-Royal complex, with its enclosed courtyards; the tallest building in the city, 1000 de la Gauchetière, with a spectacular indoor skating rink; and the high, light and luminous Centre de Commerce Mondial de Montréal.

🚣 *Montréal 6d (Ville-Marie).* Additional entrances across the city ❓ For details and maps, contact Centre Infotouriste: 1255 rue Peel, Suite 100 Montréal, Québec, H3B 4V4 ☎ 514/873-2015; 877/266-5687 (toll free)

Vieux-Montréal (Old Montréal)

Close to the river, Old Montréal is a district of narrow, cobblestoned streets and old houses. It is the original French city, now a picturesque area that you can visit either by horse-drawn carriage or on foot. Don't miss place Jacques Cartier, with its outdoor cafés, street performers and flower vendors. At the north end of the square stands Montréal's magnificent Hôtel de Ville (City Hall), built in the French Second Empire style. Across the street is the venerable Château Ramezay, built in 1705 and today housing a local history museum. Rue St-Paul is the main thoroughfare, lined by boutiques, art galleries and restaurants in fine old buildings. The most prominent is the splendid, domed Marché Bonsecours, now full of high-quality craft retailers. Finally, don't miss place d'Armes, and the Notre-Dame Basilica (► 113).

www.vieux.montreal.qc.ca

✚ Montréal 7c

🛈 Centre Infotouriste (Vieux-Montréal): 174 rue Notre-Dame Est (on corner of place Jacques Cartier) ☎ 514/873-2015

🍴 Restaurants ($–$$$) 🚇 Champ-de-Mars, place d'Armes, Square Victoria

Vieux-Port (Old Port)

The Old Port is the name given to the area beside the St. Lawrence River south of rue de la Commune, which today forms an attractive linear waterfront park with great views of the city and river. Exhibitions, activities and festivals are held here throughout the year, and there is also the Centre des Sciences de Montréal (Montréal Science Centre; ➤ 67) to visit. The 45m (145ft) **Tour de l'Horloge** (Clock Tower), beside the river, can be climbed (192 steps) for a splendid view of the city. A variety of boat trips are on offer, including jet-boat rides over the Lachine Rapids.

www.quaysoftheoldport.com

🔶 *Montréal 8d* ✉ 333 rue de la Commune Ouest, Montréal, Québec, H2Y 2E2 ☎ 514/496-7678; 800/971-7678 (toll free) 🍴 Cafés ($) 🚇 Champ-de-Mars, place d'Armes, Square Victoria

Tour de l'Horloge

✉ quai de l'Horloge, Vieux-Port de Montréal
☎ 514/496-7678; 800/971-7678 (toll free) 🕐 Late May–early Oct daily ✋ Free

QUÉBEC CITY

Citadel, seaport and provincial capital, Canada's oldest city is built on a rock above the St. Lawrence. It has a distinct European flavor, with impressive fortifications and narrow cobblestoned streets lined with gray-stone buildings. True to its claim as the birthplace of French culture in North America, Québec City offers excellent restaurants, lively cafés and a vibrant nightlife.

In 1608, Samuel de Champlain built a trading settlement at the point "where the river narrows" (the meaning of the word Québec). Over the next 150 years, his settlement grew in size and importance to become the center of all activities in New France, an empire that stretched through the Great Lakes and south to the Gulf of Mexico. In 1759, a British fleet arrived under the command of James Wolfe and scaled the great rock face that provided Québec with its natural defense. The ensuing battle on the Plains of Abraham was won by the British, deciding the fate not only of the city but of the whole continent.

Today, it is a joy to explore Québec City's Haute-Ville, at the top of the cliff, and the Basse-Ville, below it at the foot. The steep cliffs are still impressive despite the construction of port facilities at their base, and the former battlefield is now a magnificent park covering 100ha (250 acres). In 1985, the combination of fortified site and French culture gave Québec a place on UNESCO's World Heritage List, one of only two Canadian cities to receive this honor (the other is Old Town Lunenburg ► 99).

www.quebecregion.com

➕ 10E

ℹ️ 12 rue Ste-Anne, Québec G1R 3X2 ☎ 418/649-2608; 877/266-5687 (toll free)

Cathédrale Notre-Dame de Québec (Notre-Dame Cathedral)
The Roman Catholic Cathedral of Notre-Dame has a rather undistinguished neoclassical facade that belies the opulence of the interior with its gold decoration. Over the altar, a vast wooden canopy is finished in gold, as are the pulpit and the bishop's throne. On the right side, a funeral chapel honors Monsignor de Laval, the first bishop of Québec; a map of his diocese – which extended over half the continent – is etched on the floor.

This is the third cathedral on this site. The first was destroyed by British bombardments in 1759, while the second burnt down in 1922. The present cathedral stands on the same foundations and was rebuilt using the original plans.

www.patrimoine-religieux.com

✉ 16 rue de Buade ☎ 418/692-2533 ⏲ Daily from 7:30 (8:30 Sun). Closes at 4, 5 or 6pm depending on season ✋ Inexpensive ❓ Guided tours

Château Frontenac

Inextricably linked with the image of the city, this striking and
famous hotel is named after a French governor, the Comte de
Frontenac. It towers flamboyantly above its surroundings, a
magnificent structure of turrets and copper roofs. The original hotel
was built by Bruce Price for the Canadian Pacific Railway in 1893,
and its architecture gave rise to the term "château style." Even if
you are not staying here, step inside to see the interior. During
World War II, the hotel hosted the Québec Conferences, when the
Normandy landings were planned by Franklin D. Roosevelt and
Winston Churchill.

www.fairmont.com/frontenac

✉ 1 rue des Carrières ☎ 418/692-3861

🍴 Several restaurants and cafés in hotel
($–$$$) ❓ Guided tours (expensive and
popular); reservations (☎ 418/691-2166;
www.tourschateau.ca)

Citadelle (Québec Citadel)

This vast four-pointed polygon extends
over 15ha (37 acres) and remains an
active military base, home to the Royal
22e Régiment. It took the British more
than 30 years (1820–50) to complete
the vast array of earthworks and
bastions that make up the fort,
following a design by the French military
architect Vauban.

To visit the Citadel, you must join a
guided tour. Buildings bearing the
names of the various campaigns of the
Royal 22e Régiment (Vimy, the Somme
and so on) surround a huge parade
ground where military ceremonies take
place. Located in a powder magazine dating from 1750 is a
museum presenting military insignia, weapons, uniforms and an
excellent diorama showing the various battles fought at Québec.

From the Citadel, an entire network of walls and gates encircles
the old part of the city, stretching a total of 4.6km (2.8 miles).

www.lacitadelle.qc.ca

✉ Côte de la Citadelle ☎ 418/694-2815 🕐 Guided tours only; Apr daily
10–4; May–Jun daily 9–5; Jul–early Sep daily 9–6; Sep daily 9–4; Oct daily
10–3; Nov–Apr one tour daily 1:30pm. Changing of the Guard late Jun–early
Sep daily at 10am. Retreat ceremony early Jul–early Sep Fri 7pm
✋ Moderate

Holy Trinity Cathedral (Cathédrale de la Ste-Trinité)

Consecrated in 1804, this wood-framed Georgian church was the first Anglican cathedral to be built outside the British Isles. Modeled on the church of St. Martin-in-the-Fields in central London, it was paid for by King George III and still boasts a royal pew reserved for the sovereign. The light and spacious interior has box pews made of oak transported from England's royal forests. There is an impressive collection of stained glass: In the chancel, the triptych window portrays the Ascension, beside scenes of the Transfiguration and the Baptism. In the summer months, the cathedral courtyard is home to stalls selling local crafts.

http://209.160.3.218/

✉ 31 rue des Jardins ☎ 418/692-2193 ④ Mid-May to mid-Oct daily; mid-Oct to Apr Sun morning; open for services ✋ Free 🍴 Nearby ($–$$) ❓ Guided tours

Musée de la Civilisation (Museum of Civilization)

Inaugurated in 1988 and designed by architect Moshe Safdie, this building is a splendid example of how modern architecture can be integrated into the old city – incorporated within its walls is a four-story stone house, the Maison Estèbe, dating from 1751. Excavations carried out during construction unearthed many treasures. The museum is devoted to civilization in the broadest sense of the word, and the exhibitions (which change regularly) may feature life in any part of the world at any time. Among its permanent collection, there are fine examples of Québécois furniture, sculpture and crafts, as well as important First Nations artifacts.

www.mcq.org

✉ 85 rue Dalhousie ☎ 418/643-2158; 866/710-8031 (toll free) ④ Late Jun–early Sep daily 9–7; Tue–Sun 10–5, rest of year ✋ Moderate; free Tue, Nov–May and Sat 10–noon Jan–Feb 🍴 Cafeteria ($) 🚌 1 ❓ Gift store in Maison Estèbe

"SHE STRETCHETH OUT HER HAND TO THE POOR,
YEA SHE REACHETH FORTH HER HANDS TO THE NEEDY"

...RY OF GOD AND IN LOVING MEMORY OF MARY WIFE OF
...N JONES WHO ENTERED INTO REST 1ST JANUARY 1894

Place Royale

This picturesque square is in the center of the Basse-Ville (Lower Town) on the site where Samuel de Champlain built his first settlement in 1608. Today, it is lined with tall stone houses of French Regime style, with steeply pitched roofs and high chimneys (note the ladders on the roofs to enable people to climb up and sweep the chimneys). These houses were actually all rebuilt in the 1970s so that the square could take on the look it had at the time of the conquest, before it was blasted to bits by British mortar fire. A bust of King Louis XIV graces the center of the square, a copy of the original erected in 1686 that gave place Royale its name. On the west side stands the little church of Notre-Dame-des-Victoires with its distinctive steeple.

The narrow pedestrian streets around place Royale are perfect for exploration on foot. There are a number of craft stores along rue Petit-Champlain, antiques shops on rue St-Paul, and souvenir outlets just about everywhere.

🍴 Restaurants/cafés ($–$$$) ❓ Access from Upper Town by funicular (inexpensive), or by descending the "Breakneck Steps" on foot

Promenade des Gouverneurs
Best places to see, ➤ 52–53.

Terrasse Dufferin
Best places to see, ➤ 52–53.

More to see in Québec Province

CANADIAN MUSEUM OF CIVILIZATION, GATINEAU

Best places to see, ➤ 36–37.

CHARLEVOIX COAST

On the north shore of the St. Lawrence River east of Québec City
is the Charlevoix coast, where mountains sweep down to the
water's edge and villages nestle in the valleys. There are ever-
changing views of the river and shore, as well as possibilities for
whale-watching (➤ 54–55). In 1989, the Charlevoix was named a
UNESCO World Biosphere Reserve for its unique beauty.

The mountainous landscape of Charlevoix was created about
350 million years ago when a gigantic meteorite hit the Earth,
making a crater that stretches some 56km (35 miles). Highlights of
the region include Baie-St-Paul, whose beautiful location has long
been a magnet for artists, and the rural charm of Île-aux-Coudres.
www.tourisme-charlevoix.com

✚ 10E ℹ Association touristique régionale de Charlevoix: 495 boulevard
de Comporté, La Malbaie, Québec, G5A 3G3 ☎ 418/665-4454; 800/667-2276
(toll free) ❓ Ferry from St-Joseph-de-la-Rive to Île-aux-Coudres daily
(free; ☎ 418/643-7308; www.traversiers.gouv.qc.ca)

CHUTE MONTMORENCY (MONTMORENCY FALLS)

Near its junction with the St. Lawrence, the Montmorency River cascades over an 83m (272ft) cliff in an impressive waterfall. The spray it creates forms a great cone of ice up to 30m (100ft) high in the winter, known as the *pain de sucre* (sugarloaf). Tobogganing down the cone became a tradition in the 19th century and continues to this day. The falls and cliffs are illuminated at night.

Parc de la Chute Montmorency offers viewpoints at both the top and the bottom of the falls. At the top, a boardwalk takes you to a suspension bridge across the cataract that has spectacular views. At the bottom, you can walk right up to the whirlpool at the base of the falls. A cable car or steep staircase (487 steps) connects the upper and lower levels. The Manoir Montmorency at the top houses an interpretive center and restaurant.

www.sepaq.com

➕ 10E ✉ Parc de la Chute Montmorency, 2490 avenue Royal, Beauport, 12km (7.5 miles) east of Québec ☎ 418/663-3330

🕐 Upper Park: daily. Cable car and Lower Park: daily, Apr–Oct

✋ Parking fee (Apr–Oct): expensive. Cable car: expensive

🍴 Restaurant ($$) 🚌 Bus 50, 53 ❓ Craft store

EASTERN TOWNSHIPS (CANTONS DE L'EST)

Settled by Loyalists at the end of the 18th century, the Eastern Townships are a unique mixture of Anglo-Saxon ambience and French *joie de vivre*. They offer mountains rising nearly 1,000m (about 3,000ft) with a number of ski slopes, lakes perfect for boating and swimming, and quiet villages. Knowlton, near Brome Lake (famous for its

ducks), is a charming place for visitors with a variety of craft stores to browse in and restaurants to eat at. Magog is superbly set at the northern end of long and narrow Lake Memphrémagog, while the nearby **monastery of St-Benoît-du-Lac,** known for the cheeses made by its monks, has unusual multicolored buildings and a tall tower.

www.easterntownships.org

✠ 10D

🛈 Tourisme Cantons-de-l'Est: 20 rue Don-Bosco Sud, Sherbrooke, Québec, J1L 1W4 ☎ 819/820-2020; 800/355-5755 (toll free)

Abbaye St-Benoît-du-Lac

✉ St-Benoît-du-Lac, Québec, J0B 2M0. 14km (9 miles) south of Magog via Route 112 and minor road signed "Abbaye Saint-Benoît" ☎ 819/843-4080; www.st-benoit-du-lac.com 🕓 Monastery: daily. Store: Mon–Sat 9–10:45, 11:45–4:30 (to 6 Jul–Aug). Gregorian chant: at Eucharist daily 11am; and at Vespers Wed and Fri–Mon 5pm, Tue and Thu 7pm, summer; Fri–Wed 5pm, Thu 7pm, rest of year ❓ Respectable clothing required

ÎLE D'ANTICOSTI

Once a private hunting and fishing camp, the island of Anticosti in the Gulf of the St. Lawrence is today largely owned by the province of Québec and run as a nature reserve. Île d'Anticosti covers a massive 8,000sq km (3,000sq miles) and has much to offer nature lovers. There are more than 200 bird species (including bald eagles), a herd of white-tailed deer, impressive rock formations, caverns, waterfalls and the remains of about 200 shipwrecks off the rocky shores. Take the 3km (2-mile) hike up a canyon to see Vauréal Falls. Here, the river plunges 76m (249ft) into the steep-walled canyon.

www.sepaq.com

✚ 20K

🛈 Sépaq: Box 179, Port-Menier, Québec, G0G 2Y0 ☎ 418/535-0156

📧 Relais Nordik (☎ 418/723-8787; www.groupedesgagnes.com)

✖ Air Satellite (☎ 418/538-2332; www.airsatellite.com)

ÎLE D'ORLÉANS

The island of Orléans sits wedged like a giant cork in the St. Lawrence River as it widens beyond Québec City. In the early 17th century, French settlers began farming here and built the stone churches and Norman-style farmhouses that still grace its shores. In the summer months, the island becomes a vast open-air market, with fruit and vegetables on sale at roadside stands; it is especially famous for its strawberries. Route 368 makes a circular tour (about 70km/45 miles) of Île d'Orléans, giving some wonderful views of the tide-swept shores of the St. Lawrence and

of Québec City. You will pass, and can visit, the **Manoir Mauvide-Genest,** a French manor house built in 1734 that has been splendidly restored. The small stone **church of St-Pierre,** built between 1717 and 1719, is no longer consecrated but it offers a veritable museum of religious art. The island also has some excellent restaurants.

www.iledorleans.com

🕂 10E 🛈 Chambre de commerce de l'Île d'Orléans: 490 côte du Pont, St-Pierre-de-l'Île d'Orléans, Québec, G0A 4E0 ☎ 418/828-9411; 866/941-9411 (toll free)

Manoir Mauvide-Genest

✉ 1451 chemin Royal, St-Jean, Québec, G0A 3W0 ☎ 418/829-2630; www.manoirmauvidegenest.ca

🕓 Late Jun–Aug daily 10–5;
May–late Jun and Sep to mid-Oct
Sat–Sun 10–5 💷 Moderate

Église St-Pierre

✉ 1249 chemin Royale, St-Pierre-de-l'Île d'Orléans, Québec, G0A 4E0
☎ 418/828-9824 🕓 May–Oct
daily 💷 Free

LAC ST-JEAN

Located north of Québec City, this large, saucer-shaped lake (1,350sq km/521sq miles) is the source of the Saguenay River (➤ 138). The land around is flat and fertile, and is particularly known for the wild blueberries *(bleuets)* that grow on its northern shore. In the water, a species of lake trout known as *ouananiche* flourishes, highly prized by sports fishermen. Lac St-Jean is renowned as the setting for *Maria Chapdelaine*, probably the most famous novel of French Canada ever written. In Péribonka, you can learn all about this love story at the **Musée Louis-Hémon.**

Set beside Ouiatchouan Falls, the former mill town of **Val-Jalbert** has been partially restored to recreate town-life in the 1920s. Don't miss climbing to the top of the falls (via 400 steps or a cable-car ride) for the view over the lake.

✚ 17H

Musée Louis-Hémon

✉ 700 route Maria Chapdelaine, Péribonka, Québec, G0W 2G0 ☎ 418/374-2177; www.museelh.ca 🕐 Jul–Aug daily 9–5; Sep–Jun Mon–Fri 9–4 ✋ Moderate

Village historique de Val-Jalbert

✉ Route 169, Chambord, Québec, G0W 1G0 ☎ 418/275-3132; 888/675-3132 (toll free); www.sepaq.com/ct/val/en/ 🕐 May–Oct daily ✋ Expensive

LES LAURENTIDES (LAURENTIANS)

When Montréalers talk of the "Laurentides," they are referring to the mountains just north of the city where ski centers and lakes abound. St-Sauveur-des-Monts is the region's oldest resort. At Ste-Agathe-des-Monts, you can take a **boat trip** around Lac-des-Sables (Sandy Lake). The **Tremblant complex** is an astounding place surrounded by wilderness; the buildings, with their colourful, steeply pitched roofs, house boutiques, bars, restaurants and accommodations of every type.

➕ 9D

Croisières Alouette

✉ Ste-Agathe-des-Monts, Québec, J8C 3A3 ☎ 819/326-3656; www.croisierealovette.com

🕐 Early Jun to late Oct daily

✋ Expensive

Tremblant complex

ℹ Information Centre, 48 chemin de Brébeuf, Mont-Tremblant, Québec, J8E 3Bl ☎ 819/425-3300; 877/425-2434 (toll free); www.tourismemonttremblant.com 🕐 Daily 🍴 Restaurants/cafés ($$–$$$)

ROCHER PERCÉ, GASPÉSIE

Best places to see, ➤ 46-47.

SAGUENAY FJORD

For the final 60km (37 miles) before it joins the St. Lawrence, the Saguenay River passes through a deep channel in the rock gouged out by glaciers millions of years ago. Precipitous cliffs rise 500m (1,600ft) above dark waters that plunge to a depth of 240m (787ft). This stark landscape, where the hand of man is barely visible, is best appreciated by taking a **boat trip.** One highlight of the tour is Cap Trinité, so named for the three ledges that punctuate its face. On the first of these is a 9m-high (30ft) statue of the Virgin carved in 1881, an awe-inspiring sight. There are also a few viewpoints of the fjord from Routes 170 and 172, and at **Rivière-Éternité** you can follow a steep trail up to the statue of the Virgin (allow four hours return).

✚ 18H ⓘ Fédération Touristique Régionale du Saguenay-Lac-St-Jean, 412 boulevard Saguenay Est, Bureau 100, Chicoutimi, Québec G7H 7Y8 ☎ 418/543-9778; 877/253-8387 (toll-free); www.tourismesaguenaylacsaintjean.qc.ca

Boat trips

Croisières La Marjolaine: Chicoutimi (☎ 418/543-7630; 800/363-7248 toll free); www.croisieremarjolaine.com

Rivière-Éternité walk

◷ Mid-May to mid-Oct daily 🅿 Parking: expensive

STE-ANNE-DE-BEAUPRÉ

This small community on the north shore of the St. Lawrence, has been a major place of pilgrimage for Roman Catholics since the early 1600s, when Breton sailors were brought safely to land here during a storm after praying to St. Anne.

Sanctuaire Ste-Anne-de-Beaupré, the twin-spired basilica that dominates the site today, was inaugurated in 1934. Constructed of white granite in the form of a Latin cross, it has a magnificent interior with five naves, a barrel vault decorated with mosaics, and luminous stained-glass windows. Every year, a million or more pilgrims visit the basilica's north transept to pray before the statue of St. Anne holding the infant Mary. The chapel behind the statue contains a relic of the saint, which was given to the shrine by Pope John XXIII in 1960.

✚ 10E

Sanctuaire Ste-Anne-de-Beaupré

✉ 10018 avenue Royale, Ste-Anne-de-Beaupré. About 35km (22 miles) from Québec City via Highway 40 and Route 138

☎ 418/827-3781; www.ssadb.qc.ca ◷ Daily (phone for times of Mass). Museum: Early Jun to mid-Oct daily 9–5

✋ Inexpensive

🍴 Cafeteria ($)

TADOUSSAC WHALE-WATCHING CRUISES

Best places to see, ➤ 54–55.

TROIS-RIVIÈRES

An industrial center known for its pulp and paper mills, Trois-Rivières is the third city of Québec province. As it joins the St. Lawrence here, the St. Maurice River branches around two islands – hence the name Trois-Rivières (Three Rivers). Close to the river, rue des Ursulines has some of the oldest-surviving buildings, the most striking of which is the Monastère des Ursulines (Ursuline Convent) of 1697. Nearby, a waterfront promenade offers views of the port and the Laviolette Bridge across the St. Lawrence. In neighboring Cap-de-la-Madeleine is

the **Sanctuaire Notre-Dame-du-Cap,** a magnificent octagonal basilica. The church forms part of a shrine devoted to the Virgin that is visited by half a million pilgrims every year.

✚ 9D

Sanctuaire Notre-Dame-du-Cap

✉ 626 rue Notre-Dame Est, Trois Rivières, Québec, G8T 4G9 ☎ 819/374-2441; www.sanctuaire-ndc.ca

🕐 Daily 🎫 Free

🍴 Cafeteria ($) ❓ Phone for times of English Masses

HOTELS

AYER'S CLIFF
▽▽▽▽ Auberge Ripplecove Inn ($$–$$$)
In lovely gardens overlooking Lake Massawippi in the Eastern Townships. Attractive hotel with an excellent restaurant, summer terrace and outdoor pool.

✉ 700 rue Ripplecove ☎ 819/838-4296; 800/668-4296 (toll free); www.ripplecove.com

BAIE-ST-PAUL
▽▽ Aux Portes du Soleil ($–$$)
In the heart of this lovely Charlevoix town, this is a stylish place to stay with good amenities, including free wireless internet, laundry and ski and snowshoe rental.

✉ 29 rue de la Lumière (Roue 362) ☎ 418/435-3540; www.auxportesdusoleil.com

MONTRÉAL
▽▽▽ Auberge de la Fontaine ($$$)
Pleasant, small hotel in a renovated Victorian house on Lafontaine Park in Montréal's east end. Generous Continental breakfast, and guests also have access to the kitchen to prepare their own meals.

✉ 1301 rue Rachel Est ☎ 514/597-0166; 800/597-0597 (toll free); www.aubergedelafontaine.com Ⓜ Mont-Royal

▽▽▽ Château Versailles ($$$)
Luxury hotel in renovated former town houses with a modern extension across the street. Stylish bar and good restaurant.

✉ 1659 rue Sherbrooke Ouest ☎ 514/933-8111; 888/933-8111 (toll free); www.versailleshotels.com Ⓜ Guy-Concordia

▽▽▽▽ Fairmont The Queen Elizabeth ($$$)
Grand dame of downtown accommodations, opened in 1958. Connected to Montréal's Underground City (► 121). John Lennon and Yoko Ono held their famous bed-in here. Indoor pool.

✉ 900 boulevard René-Lévesque Ouest ☎ 514/861-3511; 800/257-7544 (toll free); www.fairmont.com/queenelizabeth Ⓜ Bonaventure, Peel, McGill

MONT-TREMBLANT
▼▼▼▼ Fairmont Tremblant ($$$)
Part of the enormous Tremblant resort complex, splendidly located with views of mountain and village. Rooms are standard – except for the views. Swimming pools and health club on site.

✉ 3045 chemin de la Chapelle ☎ 819/681-7000; 800/257-7544 (toll free); www.fairmont.com/tremblant

PERCÉ
▼▼▼▼ Le Mirage ($$–$$$)
Family-run hotel where every room has large windows and fabulous views of Percé's famous rock. Extensive grounds, tennis court and pool. Whale-watching boat trips can be arranged.

✉ 288 Route 132 Ouest ☎ 418/782-5151; 800/463-9011; www.hotellemirageperce.com ⊗ Closed mid-Oct to mid-May

QUÉBEC CITY
▼▼▼▼ Auberge Saint-Antoine ($$$)
In a once derelict warehouse in the Lower Town, this stylish boutique hotel has great originality and flair and includes themed suites.

✉ 8 rue St-Antoine ☎ 418/692-2211; 888/692-2211 (toll free); www.saint-antoine.com

▼▼▼▼ Fairmont Le Château Frontenac ($$$)
Dominates the Upper Town with its towers and turrets. Rooms are pleasant; those with any kind of view are expensive. Large swimming pool and spa; variety of restaurants.

✉ 1 rue des Carrières ☎ 418/692-3861; 800/257-7544 (toll free); www.fairmont.com/frontenac

▼▼ Gîte du Vieux-Bourg ($$)
This charming bed-and-breakfast, just a five-minute drive from downtown, occupies a historic stone house with a small art gallery and pool. Breakfast includes home-made bread and jam.

✉ 492 avenue Royale ☎ 418/661-0116; 866/661-0116 (toll free)

WAKEFIELD
◆◇◆ Wakefield Mill ($$)
Lovely inn in a 19th-century water mill on the La Pêche River north of Ottawa. Some rooms have exposed brick walls and hardwood floors, and some have views of the falls. Breakfast included.

✉ 60 Mill Road ☎ 819/459-1838; 888/567-1838 (toll free); www.wakefieldmill.com

RESTAURANTS

MONTRÉAL
◇◇ Alpenhaus ($$)
On the corner with busy rue Ste-Catherine. Swiss restaurant specializing in fondues, veal escalopes and entrecôte steaks.

✉ 1279 rue St-Marc ☎ 514/935-2285; www.restaurantalpenhaus.com
🕐 Mon–Wed 12–3pm, 5:30–10pm, Thu 12–10, Fri 12–10:30, Sat 4:30–10:30, Sun 5:30–10 🚇 Guy-Concordia

◇◇ Bar-B Barn ($)
A barn of a place with no frills, but the ribs are great and the chicken's not bad either.

✉ 1201 rue Guy ☎ 514/931-3811; www.barbbarn.ca 🚇 Guy-Concordia

◇◇ Café des Beaux-Arts ($$)
In the Montréal Museum of Fine Arts, this restaurant is as elegant as the surrounding art. Venison and duck are on the menu.

✉ 1384 rue Sherbrooke Ouest ☎ 514/843-3233; www.mmfa.qc.ca/services/cafe_des_beaux_arts 🕐 Tue–Sun 11:30–2:30; Wed 6–9 🚇 Guy-Concordia

◇◇ Delmo ($$)
Beautifully renovated bistro serving French classics like *moules marinère* and *bouillabaisse* and the occasional Canadian dish, such as *Bavette de bison*.

✉ 211 rue Notre-Dame Ouest ☎ 514/335-1869; www.delmo.ca
🕐 Mon–Tue 11–11, Wed–Sat 11am–midnight, Sun 5:30–11

⛝⛝⛝ Gibby's ($$$)

In fine stone buildings in Old Montréal. First and foremost a steak house, though there is also plenty of fish on the menu.

✉ 298 place d'Youville ☎ 514/282-1837; www.gibbys.com ⏱ Sun–Fri from 5pm, Sat from 4:30pm 🚇 Place Victoria

⛝⛝ House of Jazz/Maison de Jazz ($$)

This club has a long tradition of providing great ribs and the best jazz in the city.

✉ 2060 rue Aylmer ☎ 514/842-8656; www.houseofjazz.ca ⏱ Mon–Wed 11:30am–12:30am, Thu 11:30am–1:30am, Fri 11:30am–2:30am, Sat 6pm–2:30am, Sun 6pm–12:30am 🚇 McGill, Place-des-Arts

⛝⛝⛝ Milos ($$$)

Top-notch Greek restaurant with the freshest fish and vegetables in the city, flown in directly from Greece on occasion.

✉ 5357 avenue du Parc ☎ 514/272-3522; www.milos.ca ⏱ Mon–Fri 12–3, 5:30–late, Sat–Sun from 5:30pm 🚌 Bus 80 ❓ Valet parking

⛝⛝⛝ Le Piment Rouge ($$$)

Sophisticated, elegant restaurant serving excellent, well-presented Szechuan shrimp, chicken, duck and beef dishes.

✉ Le Windsor, 1170 rue Peel ☎ 514/866-7816; www.lepimentrouge.ca ⏱ Mon–Thu 11:30–11, Fri 11:30am–midnight, Sat 12–12, Sun 12–11 🚇 Peel

⛝⛝ Reuben's Deli ($)

Famous for its 10-ounce smoked-meat sandwich, Reuben's also serves prime-aged steaks, chops, burgers, salads and desserts.

✉ 1116 rue Ste-Catherine Ouest ☎ 514/866-1029; www.reubensdeli.com ⏱ Daily 6:30am–2:30am

⛝⛝ Stash Café ($–$$)

In Old Montréal. Popular bistro-type restaurant serving Polish fare such as *pirogies*, cabbage rolls, sauerkraut stew and borscht.

✉ 200 rue St-Paul Ouest ☎ 514/845-6611; www.stashcafe.com ⏱ Daily 11:30–11:30 🚇 Place d'Armes

MONT-TREMBLANT

♛ Microbrasserie Le Diable ($)

Really bustles in the evening, especially popular with skiers.
Excellent beer brewed on the spot.

✉ 117 chemin Kandahar ☎ 819/681-4546 ⏰ Daily 11:30am–3am

PERCÉ

♛♛♛ La Normandie Dining Room ($$–$$$)

Sensational location overlooking Rocher Percé. Seafood and fish
dishes with great originality and flair.

✉ 221 route 132 Ouest ☎ 418/782-2112; 800/463-0820 (toll free);
www.normandieperce.com ⏰ Dinner only. Closed Oct–early Jun

QUÉBEC CITY

♛♛ Aux Anciens Canadiens ($$)

Charming restaurant in a 17th-century house in the Upper Town.
Specializes in traditional Québec cuisine.

✉ 34 rue St-Louis ☎ 418/692-1627; www.auxancienscanadiens.qc.ca
⏰ Daily 12–9

♛♛ Au Petit Coin Breton ($$)

In the Upper Town of Old Québec. Nearly 80 varieties of crêpes.
✉ 1029 rue St-Jean ☎ 418/694-0758 ⏰ Mon–Wed 11–2, 5–9, Thu–Fri
11–10, Sat 9am–10pm

♛♛♛ Charles-Baillairgé ($$$)

Classy, popular restaurant in the Clarendon Hotel in Upper Town.
Refined cuisine and piano chamber music.

✉ Hotel Clarendon, 57 rue Ste-Anne ☎ 418/692-2480; 888/222-3304;
www.dufour.ca ⏰ Mon–Fri 7–10:30am, 11:30–2, 6–9:30, Sat–Sun 7–10:30,
6–9:30

♛♛ Le Cochon Dingue ($$)

Café-bistro par excellence in Lower Town. Excellent *frites* (fries),
mussels and desserts.

✉ 46 boulevard Champlain ☎ 418/692-2013; www.cochondingue.com
⏰ Daily 7am–11pm

▼▼▼▼ **Laurie Raphael ($$$)**

In the Old Port area of Lower Town. International cuisine with a contemporary flavor. Reservations essential.

✉ 117 rue Dalhousie ☎ 418/692-4555; www.laurieraphael.com 🕐 Tue–Fri 11:30–2, 5:30–10, Sat 5:30–10. Closed Sun, Mon

SHOPPING

SHOPPING CENTERS AND MALLS
Complexe Desjardins
On east side of downtown linked to the Underground City. Has a vast central atrium. Good choice of fashion stores.

✉ 150 rue Ste-Catherine Ouest or 175 boulevard René-Lévesque Ouest, Montreal ☎ 514/281-1870; 514/845-4636 (info-line) 🚇 Place-des-Arts

Place Laurier
West of downtown. Largest mall in Québec, with 350 stores, including Zellers, The Bay, and Sears. Food court and restaurants.

✉ 2700 boulevard Laurier, Québec City ☎ 418/651-5000

MARKETS
Atwater Market
Popular daily market selling local produce, cheese, meat, fish and bread. Acres of flowers in the spring; fruit and vegetables all summer and maple products year-round. Café.

✉ 138 avenue Atwater, Montréal ☎ 514/937-7754; www.marchpublicsmtl.com 🚇 Lionel-Groulx

Québec Public Market
In the Old Port. Sells great cheese and bread, wonderful fruit in season, maple products and flowers.

✉ 160 quai St-Andre, Quebec City ☎ 418/692-2517

CRAFTS, ANTIQUES AND OTHER SPECIALTIES
Antiquités Hier pour Demain
Québec pine furniture, woodcarvings, folk art and old toys.

✉ 914 boulevard des Laurentides, Piedmont ☎ 450/227-4231 🕐 Closed Mon–Thu

Boutique Au Bon Secours

An artisan-owned craft store in a former pharmacy selling original work by local artists, notably sandstone bird sculptures.

✉ 150 route 138 Ouest, Percé ☎ 418/782-2011 🕙 Closed Nov–Apr

Galeries d'Art Inuit Brousseau et Brousseau

Next door to the Château Frontenac. Store and gallery devoted to the works of Canada's Inuit artists and sculptors.

✉ 35 rue St-Louis, Québec City ☎ 418/694-1828; www.sculpture.artinuit.ca

Henri Henri

The hat store to beat all hat stores. Great fur hats and classic headgear for men by names such as Biltmore and Stetson.

✉ 189 rue Ste-Catherine Est, Montréal ☎ 514/288-0109; 888/388-0109; www.henrihenri.ca 🚇 St-Laurent, Berri-UQAM

Ogilvy

In business since 1866. Home to 20 or more fashion franchises. Famous for its bagpiper, who parades through the store at noon.

✉ 1307 rue Ste-Catherine Ouest, Montréal ☎ 514/842-7711 🚇 Peel

ENTERTAINMENT

CHILDREN'S ENTERTAINMENT

Parc Omega

Drive-through enclosure where you can see buffalo, moose and bear in their natural habitats. On foot, you can explore the deer enclosure and otter pool. Restaurant.

✉ 323 North Road, Montebello ☎ 819/423-5487; www.parc-omega.com 🕙 Daily 9–6 (last admission 5pm). Closes one hour earlier Nov–May
💷 Expensive

La Ronde

Québec's biggest amusement park has more than 40 rides including Goliath, one of the fastest rollercoasters in North America.

✉ 22 Chemin Macdonald, Île Sainte-Hélène, Montréal (Québec) ☎ 514/397-7777; www.laronde.com 🕙 Late May–early Sep daily; Sep–Oct weekends
💷 Expensive 🚇 Jean-Drapeau 🚌 167, 169

THEATERS AND NIGHTCLUBS

Cabaret Mado
Renowned Montréal drag queen, Mado Lamotte, owns and runs this cabaret club in the Gay Village, featuring comedy shows, drag extravaganzas, dance nights and karaoke.

✉ 1115 rue Ste-Catherine Est, Montréal ☎ 514/525-7566; www.mado.qc.ca

Café Chaos
Long-established live music venue featuring emerging local bands, DJ theme nights and free Happy Hour acoustic shows.

✉ 2031 rue St-Denis ☎ 514/844-0738; www.cafechaos.qc.ca 🚇 Berri-UQAM or Sherbrooke

Comedyworks
On the second floor of Jimbo's Pub. Improv comedy during the week and big-name shows on weekends.

✉ 1238 rue Bishop, Montréal ☎ 514/398-9661; www.comedyworksmontreal.com 🚇 Guy-Concordia, Lucien L'Allier

House of Jazz/Masion de Jazz
See page 144.

Grand Théâtre du Québec
Home to the Opéra du Québec and the Québec Symphony Orchestra. Annual program of dance, music and French theater.

✉ 269 boulevard René-Lévesque Est, Québec City ☎ 418/643-8131; www.grandtheatre.qc.ca

Place des Arts
Montréal's major performing arts center, with a concert hall, four theaters, and the Museum of Contemporary Art. Classical music, opera, ballet and live theater year-round.

✉ 175 rue Ste-Catherine Ouest, Montréal ☎ 514/842-2112; 866/842-2112 (toll-free); www.pda.qc.ca 🚇 Place-des-Arts

Ontario

Ontario is Canada's heartland economically, politically and culturally; it is also the most populous of all the provinces and the richest. The waters of four of the five Great Lakes wash its shores and it takes its name from one of them. In fact, the word Ontario actually means "shining waters," an apt description of a province that includes 200,000sq km (70,000sq miles) of lakes.

The beauty of such natural regions as the Thousand Islands and Georgian Bay is closely associated with water, and Ontario's major cities are all located either beside a lake or next to a large river. Thunder Bay lies on Lake Superior, Sault Ste. Marie is on the St. Mary's River, Ottawa has an impressive site on the river of the same name, and Toronto – the province's capital and Canada's largest city and financial center – sits majestically on the northern shore of Lake Ontario. Last but not least, the province boasts the magnificent spectacle of Niagara Falls, one of the world's great tourist attractions.

OTTAWA

As befits a nation's capital, Ottawa has its fair share of imposing architecture: The Parliament Buildings are a masterpiece of Gothic fantasy and some of the national museums are splendidly housed. But visitors tend to remember the beautiful drives by the river, the canal (which becomes a vast skating rink in the winter), the tulips in May and the stalls of fresh produce at the Byward Market.

Ottawa wasn't originally intended to be the capital. It started life as a raucous lumber town and was taken over by the military when the Rideau Canal was built in the 1820s. Queen Victoria considered both Montréal and York (now Toronto) too close to the U.S. border to be the new capital of her colony, so in 1857 she chose "Bytown" instead. This choice did not please everyone, and the city was soon nicknamed "Westminster in the Wilderness" by its detractors. The inhabitants, however,

renamed their home after the river on which it stands. And since the Ottawa River marks the boundary between the provinces of Ontario and Québec, between English-speaking and French-speaking Canada, it did indeed prove to be a good choice.

Today, Ottawa is very much a city of government, and is not ruled by the temples of

finance as are Toronto and Montréal. Instead, the highrise buildings contain government departments and some of the most expensive homes here are owned by civil servants. But Ottawa is not a contrived place created to impress people with the greatness of Canada. In many ways, it defies the image many people have of what a capital city ought to be. It is in the end quintessentially Canadian.

✚ 9D

National Capital Commission Infocentre

✉ 90 Wellington Street (opposite Parliament Buildings), Ottawa, Ontario, K1P 5A1 ☎ 613/239-5000; 800/465-1867 (toll free); www.canadascapital.gc.ca 🕐 Daily

Canada Aviation Museum

Housed in a huge triangular hangar, the Canada Aviation Museum is home to the most comprehensive collection of aircraft in Canada which illustrate the story of aeronautical history. Many deem it to be the most impressive collection of vintage aircraft in the world, which is not too surprising when one considers how important airplanes have been in opening up Canada.

The Walkway of Time takes you on a journey through the different eras of aviation development. You can relive the adventures of Canada's bush pilots and see examples of the De Havilland Beaver (this plane was the prototype of a total of 1,600 that were built), and the Twin Otter, two of Canada's most important contributions to international aviation. You can even venture on a virtual-reality hang glider!

www.aviation.technomuses.ca

✉ 11 Aviation Parkway ☎ 613/993-2010; 800/463-2038 (toll free) ⏰ May–early Sep daily 9–5; early Sep–Apr Wed–Sun 10–5 ✋ Moderate; free 4–5pm. Parking: free 🍴 Café ($) ❓ Aeronautica gift shop

Canada Science and Technology Museum

This fascinating museum is devoted to the ingenuity of Canadian inventions, and every aspect of the scientific spectrum is featured – from the snowmobile to the Canadarm (part of the space shuttle). With its profusion of waterways, Canada was largely explored by canoe, and the museum has an excellent display detailing its development. The Locomotive Hall is another highlight, with an incredible display of huge and powerful locomotives. There's a splendid account of Canada in space, which features a popular simulator. In it you can "travel" to Mars to save a colony whose generator has been damaged by meteorites.

www.sciencetech.technomuses.ca

✉ 1867 St. Laurent Boulevard ☎ 613/991-3044; 866/442-4416 (toll free) ⏰ May–early Sep daily 9–5; early Sep–Apr Tue–Sun 9–5 ✋ Moderate; additional charge for the Simex Virtual Voyages™ Simulator

Canadian War Museum

From the early days of New France through two world wars to present-day peacekeeping duties for the United Nations, Canada has had an interesting military history. This is splendidly brought to life at the Canadian War Museum through the use of life-size dioramas and displays. Highlights include memorabilia from the Battle of Vimy Ridge in 1917, the D-Day landings of 1944 (including a Mercedes-Benz car used by Adolf Hitler), and Korea in the 1950s. A more modern acquisition is the Iltis jeep used by Canadian peacekeepers wounded in Bosnia.

www.civilization.ca

✉ 1 Vimy Place ☎ 819/776-8600; 800/555-5621 (toll free) 🕐 May to mid-Oct daily 9–6 (to 9pm Thu; also to 9pm Fri Jul-early Sep); mid-Oct to Apr Tue–Sun 9–5 (to 9pm Thu) ✋ Moderate; free Thu 4–9, Jul 1 and Nov 11 🍴 The Mess ($), May to mid-Oct ❓ Gift store

National Gallery of Canada

Masterpiece of architect Moshe Safdie, the National Gallery of Canada is a visually stunning building with a tower whose glittering prisms echo the Gothic turrets of the Parliamentary Library across the Rideau Canal. It occupies a splendid site in the heart of the city with wonderful views of the Canadian Parliament. Inside, the Great Hall has more splendid views, and the long, elegant galleries, courtyards and skylights diffuse natural light throughout the building.

The gallery is home to more than 1,500 works of Canadian art, from the religious works of New France to today's contemporary presentations. Don't miss the Rideau Chapel, which has a neo-Gothic fan-vaulted ceiling; the Croscup Room, with naive murals painted in Nova Scotia; and the rooms of Inuit art that are hidden away in the basement. The gallery also has an important European collection and hosts major temporary exhibitions.

www.national.gallery.ca

✉ 380 Sussex Drive ☎ 613/990-1985; 800/319-2787 (toll free)

🕐 Daily 10–5 (until 8 pm Thu); closed Mon Oct–Apr

🍴 Restaurant ($$), cafeteria ($) ✋ Permanent collection: moderate; free Thu 5–8 and Jul 1. Special exhibitions: expensive. On-site pay parking: $2:50 half-hour, $12 all day ❓ Guided tours. Bookstore

Parliament Hill

The three buildings of the Canadian Parliament stand on a high bluff above the Ottawa River and are commonly referred to as Parliament Hill. Neo-Gothic in their architectural inspiration, their copper roofs, carved stonework, turrets and towers are nothing if not picturesque. The East and West blocks (which house offices) date from the 1860s, while the Centre Block (which houses the House of Commons and the Senate) was rebuilt after a fire in 1916. At the center of the latter is the Peace Tower, 91m (300ft) high and added in 1927 as a monument to Canadians killed during World War I; it contains a carillon of 53 bells.

From Wellington Street, walk around the exterior of the buildings (you will pass the Info-Tent, where tours of the interior start in summer). There are wonderful views of the Ottawa River and Gatineau, Québec, as well as monuments to Canadian politicians. Overlooking the river is the Gothic structure that houses the Parliamentary Library, the only part of the Centre Block to survive the 1916 fire.

www.canadascapital.gc.ca

🕓 Daily 🛈 National Capital Commission Infocentre: 90 Wellington Street (opposite Parliament Buildings) ☎ 613/239-5000; 800/465-1867 (toll free) 🖐 Free ❓ Guided tours leave from Info-Tent. Mid-May to late Jun daily 9–5; late Jun–early Sep daily 9–8; from Visitor Welcome Centre in Centre Block rest of year. Changing of the Guard: late Jun–late Aug daily 10am. Sound and light shows: late Jun–late Aug daily ☎ 613/239-5000 for times and language ❓ Visitors have to go

through a security check before
entering Parliament buildings

Rideau Canal and Locks

Today, this canal – built in the
1820s as a military route
between Ottawa and Kingston
(► 170) – forms an attractive
linear park as it cuts right
through the heart of the capital.
You can stroll or join the
joggers beside it, or take a boat
cruise along it. In the winter
months, it becomes a 7.8km-
long (4.8-mile) skating rink.
Between Parliament Hill and
the Château Laurier Hotel, the
canal descends to the Ottawa
River via a series of eight flight
locks. In the shadow of serious
parliamentary business, it's
diverting to watch the pleasure
craft cruising up and down.
www.canadascapital.gc.ca
🚹 National Capital Commission
Infocentre: 90 Wellington Street
(opposite Parliament Buildings)
☎ 613/239-5000; 800/465-1867
(toll free); 613/239-5234 (ice
conditions) ❓ Boat cruises
(expensive) run mid-May to mid-Oct
daily: Paul's Boat Lines Ltd
(☎ 613/225-6781; 613/235-8409;
www.paulsboatcruises.com)

TORONTO

Set on the north shore of Lake Ontario, and with a skyline dominated by the CN Tower, Toronto is an amazingly diverse city. It is a great North American metropolis, vastly wealthy and powerful in financial terms, with a population that is both eclectic and ethnically mixed. There are districts where you are transported to China, Korea or India; to Italy, Portugal or Greece; to Poland, Hungary or Ukraine; and to Chile, San Salvador or Jamaica.

In 1793, Governor John Graves Simcoe decided to locate the new capital of Upper Canada on a swampy site north of Lake Ontario. He called it York after one of the sons of George III, but it was soon nicknamed "Muddy York" because of the state of its streets. In 1813, the Americans burned it to the ground, but it rose from the ashes to become, by the end of the 19th century, a bastion of Anglo-Saxon rectitude. By the 1920s, it was known as "Toronto the Good" and Prohibition reigned.

After World War II, the Ontario capital slowly started to blossom. Immigrants poured in from every corner of the world, providing a stimulating mix of social activities and making it one of the world's most ethnically varied cities. Gradually, Toronto took over from Montréal as Canada's economic heart. In the downtown area close to the lake, the country's great fiscal institutions have vied to build bigger and more impressively than one another. As a result, modern-day Toronto boasts an attractive skyline and some spectacular contemporary architecture. It offers a range of interesting attractions for the visitor, including some innovative cultural institutions housing collections to rival those of the world's greatest museums, again displaying some stunning modern architecture.

www.torontotourism.com

✚ 7B

ℹ 207 Queens Quay West, Toronto, Ontario, M5J 1A7

☎ 416/203-2600; 800/499-2514 (toll free) 🕒 Mon–Fri during business hours

Art Gallery of Ontario

In November 2008 the expanded and transformed AGO reopened, marking the end of an ambitious and inspirational project that has added more than 9,000sq m (97,000sq ft) of gallery space and renovated some 17,600sq m (190,000sq ft) of the existing building, at a cost of $254 million. The stunning new building, by internationally acclaimed architect Frank Gehry, has vastly enhanced what was already one of the finest art galleries in the world, flooding the building with natural light and offering tantalizing glimpses of some of its treasures to passersby on the street.

The project was prompted by the gift of the

magnificent art collection of Ken Thomson, including important European masterpieces and pivotal works by leading Canadian artists. These works add to the gallery's already remarkable collections, which span all periods, genres and media.

The many highlights of the gallery include the Henry Moore Sculpture Centre, housing the world's largest public collection – some 900 pieces – of the works of the great British sculptor.

www.ago.net

✚ *Toronto 2d* ✉ 317 Dundas Street West ☎ 416/979-6648 ⏰ Wed–Fri 12–9, Sat–Sun 10–5:30 💲 Expensive; free Wed 6–9pm 🍽 Restaurant ($$), café ($) Ⓟ St. Patrick 🚌 Dundas streetcar 505 ❓ Gift and book store

CN Tower

Best places to see, ➤ 40–41.

Distillery District

In 2003 a lively new district burst onto the Toronto scene, a National Historic Site created out of the abandoned complex of the old Gooderham and Worts distillery. Established in the 1830s, the distillery was at one time producing more than 2 million gallons of whiskey a year, but the business declined during the 20th century and eventually closed in 1990.

Now, the 44 splendidly preserved Victorian industrial buildings, linked by cobblestoned streets and covering more than 5 hectares (13 acres), are home to artists' studios and galleries, upscale boutiques, theaters, restaurants, cafés and cultural venues, including the Young Centre for the Perfoming Arts. There's a farmers' market every Sunday and a full program of events throughout the year. In common with the rest of Toronto (aka "Hollywood North") the district is a popular filming location.

www.thedistillerydistrict.com

✚ *Toronto 4b (off map)* ✉ Mill Street ☎ 416/364-1177 🍽 Restaurants and cafés on site ($–$$$) Ⓟ Castle Frank, then bus 65A south, or Union Station then bus 🚌 65A, 72, 172; King streetcar 504 to Parliament Street

Harbourfront Centre

Over the past 30 years, the city's industrial docklands have been renovated to create a recreational and cultural attraction that draws thousands of visitors every year. Part of Harbourfront's popularity lies in the infinite variety of the activites it offers. Some go there just to wander along the waterfront and to admire the views; others go to shop at the chic stores of Queens Quay Terminal, or to eat at one of the restaurants there. Some head for York Quay Terminal, with studios housing craftspeople at work; still others take part in one of the many cultural events held here.

www.harbourfrontcentre.com

✚ *Toronto 3a* ✉ South of Queens Quay West between York Street and Spadina Avenue ☎ 416/973-4000 🕐 Daily 10am–11pm (to 9pm Sun) ✋ Free. Parking: expensive 🍴 Restaurants and cafés ($–$$$) Ⓜ Union or Spadina, then streetcar 🚋 Harbourfront streetcar 509, 510

Kensington Market

The warren of small streets around Kensington Avenue offers an amazing potpourri of businesses. Houses have been converted into shops, and casual restaurants and stores spill out onto the street. Chilean butchers, Italian fishmongers and Portuguese spice merchants stand cheek by jowl with Jamaican fast-food stands and Laotian eateries. You can buy spices, unusual vegetables, fish, cheeses and breads. With its incredible cacophony of sounds it may

seem chaotic, but if you want to buy carpets, secondhand furniture or vintage clothing, there's no place like it.

www.kensington-market.ca

✚ *Toronto 1d* ✉ North of Dundas Street West and west of Spadina Avenue ⏰ Daily 🍴 Variety of eateries ($–$$) Ⓜ St. Patrick 🚌 Dundas, Spadina or Bathurst streetcar

Ontario Place

Ontario Place is a popular summer amusement park located on the Toronto waterfront. Visitors can chose from 30 different rides, a huge water park called Soak City and Canada's largest soft-play climbing structure. There's the Rush River raft ride, a mega maze, bumper boats, the Mars Simulator ride and the wonderful Children's Village. A geodesic dome houses the Cinesphere, with an IMAX movie theater; the Molson Amphitheatre offers star-studded shows; and the Atlantis Pavilions have a nightclub that offers great views of Toronto's skyline from its rooftop patio.

www.ontarioplace.com

✚ *Toronto 1a (off map)* ✉ 955 Lakeshore Boulevard West ☎ 416/314-9900; 866/663-4386 (toll free) ⏰ Jun–Aug daily; May and Sep some weekends. Cinesphere, Molson Amphitheatre and Atlantis Pavilions: daily ✋ Parking: very expensive 🍴 Restaurants ($–$$) Ⓜ Union Station then streetcar 509 west to Exhibition; Bathurst, then streetcar 511 south to Exhibition Place; Wilson or Dufferin, then bus 29 south 🚃 GO Train to Exhibition Place 🚌 29; streetcars 509, 511 to Exhibition Place

Ontario Science Centre

A multimillion dollar project has made this world-leading science

center even better, with an impressive range of 21st-century features that involve visitors of all ages. There are lots of fun "learn-through-play" areas for younger children, plus the inspirational Weston Family Innovation Centre that is designed to enthrall and challenge teens and young adults, from making music and fashion design to ecological problem-solving. There's also an OMNIMAX theater with a giant 24m (80ft) wraparound screen where you can be blown away by 13,000 watts of digital sound.

www.ontariosciencecentre.ca

✚ *Toronto 4f (off map)* ✉ 770 Don Mills Road ☎ 416/696-3127; OMNIMAX: 416/696-1000 🕔 Daily 10–5 (to 6 in summer; extended hours for March Break); closed Dec 25 ✋ Expensive; parking charge: $8 🍴 Galileo's Bistro restaurant ($$–$$$), Lobby café and Valley Marketplace cafeteria ($) 🚇 Eglinton, then Eglinton bus 34 east or Pape, then Don Mills bus 25 ❓ Mastermind Toys gift store

Royal Ontario Museum

Already Canada's largest museum, the Royal Ontario Museum (ROM) now has a massive 7,500sq m (80,000sq ft) of additional exhibition space: The Michael Lee-Chin Crystal. Daniel Libeskind's stunning extension, inspired by the museum's mineral collection, is in the form of a giant crystal that bursts out of the original building in a riot of glass and metal prisms, angled over Bloor Street and up into the skyline.

Inside, the breathtaking collections, amounting to some 6 million items, encompass world cultures from every continent and span the ages of civilization. Highlights include one of the foremost collections of Chinese temple art in the world, the excellent South Asia gallery and medieval European collections. Canada is also superbly represented, including a comprehensive insight into First Nations culture and the lives of the early European settlers.

The museum is also famous for its natural history collections, the most popular being the magnificent Age of Dinosaurs exhibit, which features 25 fully mounted skeletons and more than 300 other speciments, plus hundreds of fossils. Interactive information stations complete the fascinating insight into the past.

www.rom.on.ca

🚇 *Toronto 3f* ✉ 100 Queen's Park (main entrance on Bloor Street)
☎ 416/586-8000 🕐 Daily 10–5:30 (to 9:30pm Fri); closed Dec 25 and Jan 1
✋ Expensive; free after 4:30 Wed, half price Fri 4:30–9:30pm 🍴 Restaurant ($$$), cafeteria ($) 🏛 Museum ❓ Free guided tours daily. Gift store

Toronto Islands

An urban oasis close to downtown Toronto, these islands provide a pleasant retreat from the summer heat of the city, as a light refreshing breeze blows in off the lake. For the visitor, they offer absolutely stunning views of the Toronto skyline, as well as beaches, picnic sites, walking and cycling trails, marinas, various sporting facilities and the Centreville amusement park and Franklin Children's Garden Farm for children.

Centre Island is the busiest area. From the ferry terminal here, it is about a 45-minute walk to either Hanlan's Point at the western end or to Ward's Island in the east. En route to Hanlan's Point, you will pass the Gibraltar Point Lighthouse which is reputedly the oldest surviving structure in Toronto (1806).

www.toronto.ca/parks/island

➕ *Toronto 4a (off map)* ☎ Toronto Parks: 416/392-1111 (general information); 416/397-2628 (island information line) 🕐 Daily (no winter ferry service to Centre Island) 🎫 Ferry fare: moderate 🍴 Rectory Café, Ward's Island ($–$$), seasonal snack bars ($), picnic sites 🚢 From foot of Bay Street to Hanlan's Point, Centre Island, and Ward's Island ☎ 416/392-8193

❓ Bicycle rentals, public beaches

Toronto Zoo

Covering 287ha (710 acres), Canada's foremost zoo allows visitors to see animals from different areas of the world in settings that are as natural as possible. The African Savanna reserve is home to elephants, giraffes, antelopes and white rhinos, while a troop of gorillas provides entertainment in a separate pavilion. Kangaroos, wombats and pythons star in the Australasian enclosure, and in the Indomalayan pavilion is tropical forest with exotic birds and an orangutan family. The Canadian Domain houses native animals. There's also an interactive kids' zoo, Splash Island water park and entertainment at the Waterside Theatre.

www.torontozoo.com

➕ *Toronto 4f (off map)* ✉ Meadowvale Road, Scarborough ☎ 416/392-5929 🕓 Mid-Mar to mid-Oct daily 9–6 (to 7:30 mid-May to early Sep); mid-Oct to mid-Mar daily 9:30–4:30 💰 Expensive. Parking charge Mar–Oct 🍴 Fast food ($), picnic sites 🚇 Kennedy then bus 86A; Don Mills then Sheppard East bus 85, 85A or 85B ❓ Zoomobile mini-train service around the zoo. Large animal-oriented gift store

Yorkville

Back in the 1960s, Yorkville was the center of the city's counter-culture. The rents were low and the drug culture prevailed. But times have changed, and it has now become Toronto's most

fashionable neighborhood with some of the most expensive real estate in Canada. Outdoor cafés flourish in the summer months and Yorkville and Cumberland avenues are packed with the rich and beautiful shopping in the *haute couture* boutiques and exclusive galleries.

➕ *Toronto 2f* 🚇 Bay

More to see in Ontario

ALGONQUIN PROVINCIAL PARK

Algonquin Provincial Park is the very essence of wilderness. Despite its location in central Ontario within a day's drive of both Ottawa and Toronto, the only way to explore the interior is by canoe or on foot. From the visitor center on Highway 60, a number of trails head for the interior. Algonquin offers splendid opportunities for viewing wildlife. White-tailed deer and bears can be seen, as can moose in spring, early summer and during the mating season. Algonquin is famous for its wolves, which are often heard but only rarely seen – in August, the park staff organize "wolf howling" expeditions. More than 260 species of bird have been recorded, including the common loon, which can be found nesting on just about every lake.

www.algonquinpark.on.ca

✚ 7C ✉ Box 219, Whitney, Ontario, K0J 2M0

☎ 705/633-5572 🕐 Daily 🍴 Food services 🐾 Inexpensive

❓ Accommodations available, including campsites

GEORGIAN BAY

Although it is part of Lake Huron, Georgian Bay is almost a lake in its own right thanks to the Bruce Peninsula and Manitoulin Island, which nearly enclose it. The southern part of the bay is blessed with sandy beaches where resorts proliferate. The northern and eastern shorelines are very indented; offshore here are thousands of small rocky islands of smooth granite topped with windswept trees. Scenic boat tours are available. The twin harbors at Tobermory, at the tip of the Bruce Peninsula, are full of pleasure craft in the summer months. A ferry crosses from here to Manitoulin Island. Just off Manitoulin is Flowerpot Island, famous for its picturesque sea stacks – visitors can take a cruise around the island and/or land and hike along its coast (4.3km/2.7 miles) to see these rock pillars.

www.georgianbaytourism.on.ca

🚩 6C 🛈 980 King Street, Midland, Ontario L4R 4K3 ☎ 800/263-7745

🚢 Ferry between Tobermory and Manitoulin Island (May to mid-Oct daily)

☎ 519/371-2354; 800/265-3163 (toll free) ✋ Access to Flowerpot Island: moderate. Boat cruises: expensive

KINGSTON

Located at the eastern end of Lake Ontario, Kingston is a gracious city and is home to Queens University and the Royal Military College. Its grandiose City Hall was built in 1844 as a possible Parliament when the city hoped to become the capital.

An important British naval base in the early 19th century, it was equipped with a dockyard and an impressive stone fortress. Today restored to its full splendor, **Fort Henry** offers an excellent picture of military life in the mid-19th century, with barracks, kitchens, guard room and powder magazine, all animated by costumed interpreters and a trained troop who perform military displays.

www.kingstoncanada.com

✚ 8C ℹ Kingston Tourist Information Office: 209 Ontario Street, Kingston, Ontario, K7L 2Z1 ☎ 613/548-4415; 888/855-4555 (toll free) ❓ Boats leave Kingston to cruise the Thousand Islands (➤ 176)

Fort Henry National Historic Site

www.forthenry.com

✉ County Road 2, P.O. Box 213, Kingston, Ontario, K7L 4V8 ☎ 613/542-7388 ⏰ Mid-May to early Oct daily 10–5 💵 Expensive 🍴 Soldiers' canteen ($) ❓ Garrison Store (gift store); Fort Henry Guard sunset ceremonies: Wed, Jul–Aug (phone for details of other performances)

KLEINBURG

The small community of Kleinburg in the Humber River valley has the splendid **McMichael Canadian Art Collection** given to the province of Ontario by Robert and Signe McMichael. Located in a series of sprawling log buildings, the gallery is devoted entirely to Canadian art and features the finest collection in existence of works by the Group of Seven. In the 1920s, these artists sought to create a Canadian way of representing their country on its own terms rather than in the standard European tradition.

The galleries are arranged so that you can just ramble around admiring the works while at the same time looking out of the large windows at scenery similar to that depicted in the canvases. The McMichael also owns a superb collection of First Nations art, including sculptures by West Coast peoples, the striking prints of Norval Morrisseau and Inuit soapstone carvings.

www.kleinburgvillage.com

✚ 7B

McMichael Canadian Art Collection

✉ 10365 Islington Avenue, Kleinburg, Ontario L0J 1C0 ☎ 905/893-1121; 888/213-1121 (toll free); www.mcmichael.com ⏰ Daily 10–4; (to 5 Sun early May–late Oct); closed Dec 25

✋ Expensive. Parking charge: $5

🍴 Restaurant ($$) ❓ Gallery shop

NIAGARA FALLS

Best places to see, ➤ 44–45.

NIAGARA-ON-THE-LAKE

Settled by Loyalists after the American Revolution,
Niagara-on-the-Lake was burned to the ground by the
Americans during the War of 1812. It was rebuilt soon
afterwards, and today is a quiet town of gracious
homes and tree-lined streets far from the commotion
of Niagara Falls. It is also at the center of the
flourishing Niagara wine industry (➤ 15).

Niagara-on-the-Lake is renowned for its annual
Shaw Festival (➤ 186) and also for **Fort George.**
Built in the 1790s, this garrison played an important
role in the War of 1812 and has been restored to reflect that time.
www.niagaraonthelake.com

🔴 8B 🛈 Niagara-on-the-Lake Chamber of Commerce: 26 Queen Street,
Niagara-on-the-Lake, Ontario, L0S 1J0 ☎ 905/468-1950

Fort George National Historic Park

✉ 26 Queen Street ☎ 905/468-4257; www.pc.gc.ca/lhn-nhs/on/fortgeorge

🕐 May–Oct daily 10–5, Apr and Nov Sat–Sun 10–5 🚶 Moderate

🍴 Restaurants in town ($–$$$)

NIAGARA PARKWAY

The Niagara Parkway follows the river on its course from Lake Erie to Lake Ontario. Put in place in 1923 by the Niagara Parks Commission, the parkway protects the environment around the falls from commercial development. Along its course drivers can enjoy the spectacle of the falls for themselves as well as more tranquil sections and the **Niagara Parks Botanical Gardens.**

At **Queenston Heights,** the Niagara Parkway crosses the Niagara Escarpment, a massive ridge of sedimentary rock towering 106m (350ft) above the river. The escarpment provides good soil and protection for the farmlands of the area.

www.niagaraparks.com

➕ 8B ✉ Niagara Parks Commission

ℹ Welcome Centers and information points at various locations ☎ 905/371-0254; 877/642-7275 (toll free)

Niagara Parks Botanical Gardens and Queenston Heights Park

☎ 905/371-0254 🕐 Daily 💲 Free

🚌 Niagara People Mover bus (Mar–Dec)

POINT PELEE NATIONAL PARK

At 42 degrees north (the same latitude as northern California and Rome), Point Pelee has a plant and animal life unique in Canada. This triangular peninsula in Lake Erie is what is known as a "migration trap." Thousands of birds and the monarch butterfly are among the creatures drawn here during the spring and fall migrations.

The Park Visitor Centre offers a wealth of information but be sure not to miss the special exhibit at Point Pelee (the most southerly tip of the Canadian mainland) that provides more information on bird migration.

www.pc.gc.ca/pn-np/on/pelee

➕ 6A ✉ 407 Monarch Lane, RR1, Leamington, Ontario, N8H 3V4 ☎ 519/322-2365; 888/773-8888 (toll free)
🕐 Daily 6am–10pm (7–7 Nov–Mar) 👣 Moderate
🍽 Cattail Café on the marsh boardwalk ❓ Tip of Canadian mainland accessible by private vehicle Nov–Mar; by free shuttle bus Apr–Oct. Bookstore in visitor center

SAULT STE. MARIE

"The Soo" is located on the north side of the St. Mary's River, which connects Lake Superior to Lake Huron. In just 1.5km (1 mile), this river drops more than 6m (21 ft) in a string of turbulent rapids (*sault* in French). Today, one of the busiest canal systems in the world is in place here, incorporating some of the world's longest locks (411m/1,350ft) so that shipping can make the passage. **Boat cruises** offer visitors the chance of viewing this last stage of the St. Lawrence Seaway, where ships complete their journey from the Atlantic into

the heart of the continent. The Algoma railroad offers day trips
into the wilderness to the north of Sault Ste. Marie (➤ 62).
www.saulttourism.com

✚ 5C ✉ Tourism Sault Ste. Marie: 99 Foster Drive, Sault Ste. Marie,
Ontario, P6A 5X6 ☎ 705/759-5442; 800/461-6020 (toll free)

Lock Tours Canada Boat Cruises

✉ Roberta Bondar Park, Sault Ste. Marie ☎ 705/253-9850; 877/226-3665
(toll free); www.locktours.com 🕐 Late May–Sep daily 12:30 and 3 (also 6
late Jun–Aug); first 2 weeks in Oct daily 12:30 ✋ Expensive

SUDBURY

Sudbury sits on the largest-known source of nickel and copper ores in the world. First and foremost a mining center, it is dominated by a 380m-high (1,250ft) chimney, known as "Super Stack." Most people make the trek to Sudbury to visit Science North (► 48–49), but there is also a fascinating mine to see here. **Dynamic Earth** is housed in the former Big Nickel Mine. An elevator transports you to the bottom of a rock chasm (20m/65ft down). As you descend, a presentation is projected onto the rock face. During the tour, former miners recount stories from Sudbury's mining history. At the surface, an exhibition center explains the importance of the crater in which Sudbury is located.

www.city.greatersudbury.on.ca

✚ 6C ✉ City of Greater Sudbury: Station A, 200 Brady Street, Sudbury, Ontario, P3A 5P3 ☎ 705/671-2489

Dynamic Earth

✉ 122 Big Nickel Road ☎ 705/523-4629; 800/461-4898 (toll free); www.dynamicearth.ca ⊙ Mid-Mar to late Apr daily 10–4; late Apr–late Jun daily 9–5; late Jun–early Sep daily 9–6 ✋ Expensive (combined ticket with Science North available)

THOUSAND ISLANDS

As it leaves Lake Ontario, the St. Lawrence River passes a multitude of islands, some large and forested, others simply rocky outcrops supporting a few pine trees. The exposed is Precambrian granite, with a pinkish hue in places, combined with the sparkling waters and surrounding greenery, makes this region delightful.

www.1000islandsgananoque.com

✚ 9C ✉ Chamber of Commerce, 10 King Street East, Gananoque, Ontario, K7G 1E6 ☎ 613/382-3250; 800/561-1595 (toll free)

THUNDER BAY

Thunder Bay is located deep in the heart of the continent on the northwest shore of Lake Superior, at the head of navigation to the Great Lakes from the Atlantic. As such, it has been an important port and place of exchange. In the early 19th century, furs dominated the local economy, while most recently grain was handled here – huge elevators still dominate the skyline today.

The fur trade era is brilliantly recreated at **Old Fort William,** where you step back to the year 1815 when the canoes of the voyageurs filled the waterways, and a great rendezvous was held here every year to exchange pelts for trade goods. The reconstructed fort is huge, with more than 40 buildings, and is peopled by a whole cast of colorful characters.

www.visitthunderbay.com

✚ 3D

ℹ Tourism Thunder Bay, Terry Fox Centre, Highway 11–17, Thunder Bay, Ontario, P7C 5K4 ☎ 807/625-3960; 800/667-8386 (toll free)

Old Fort William Historical Park

✉ 1350 King Road, Thunder Bay, Ontario, P7K 1L7 ☎ 807/473-2344; www.fwhp.ca 🕐 Mid-May to mid-Oct daily 10–5 💰 Expensive; moderate in May and Oct, when activities are reduced 🍴 Café ($) ❓ Trading Post gift store

UPPER CANADA VILLAGE

This imaginative and fun complex, located beside the St. Lawrence River, reproduces early life in what is now Ontario. It is not a museum as such, but a recreation of a slice of life as it was 150 years ago. At the time, this area of Ontario was settled by Loyalists, who worked hard to establish prosperous farms and businesses. While strolling round the village, you will meet the inhabitants as they go about their daily tasks such as cheese-making, tending livestock and spinning wool.

www.uppercanadavillage.com

🔀 9C ✉ 13740 County Road 2, Morrisburg, Ontario, K0C 1X0 ☎ 613/543-4328; 800/437-2233 (toll free) 🕐 Mid-May to early Oct daily 9:30–5 ✋ Expensive 🍽 Willard's Hotel ($$), Harvest Barn Restaurant ($), Village Café ($) ❓ Village Store – excellent Canadian gift shop

HOTELS

GANANOQUE
☼☼☼ Gananoque Inn ($$–$$$)
Historic inn with spectacular views beside the St. Lawrence. Rooms are located in several different buildings, some of them on the waterfront. Dining room with exceptionally good food.
✉ 550 Stone Street South ☎ 613/382-2165; 800/465-3101 (toll free); www.gananoqueinn.com

HAMILTON
☼☼☼ Visitors Inn ($$–$$$)
Above-average hotel in the city center. Rooms are stylish and some have kitchenettes. Indoor pool, fitness center; dining room.
✉ 649 Main Street West ☎ 905/529-6979; 800/387-4620 (toll free); www.visitorsinn.com

KINGSTON
☼☼ Peachtree Inn ($$)
Excellent location with easy access to the city, highways and shopping. Spacious rooms and loft-style suites.
✉ 1187 Princess Street ☎ 613/546-4411; 800/706-0698 (toll free); www.peachtreeinn.net

NIAGARA FALLS
☼☼ ☼☼ Sheraton Fallsview ($$$)
The best place in Niagara Falls – it is a high-rise structure with fabulous views of both the Canadian and American falls. Indoor pool, dining room (with views) and very high prices.
✉ 6755 Fallsview Boulevard ☎ 905/374-1077; 800/618-9059 (toll free); www.fallsview.com

NIAGARA-ON-THE-LAKE
☼☼ ☼☼ Pillar and Post Inn ($$$)
Lovely old inn (1890) in the heart of Niagara-on-the-Lake. Rooms are pleasantly Victorian in atmosphere. Full spa; excellent food.
✉ 48 John Street ☎ 905/468-2123; 888/669-5566 (toll free); www.vintage-hotels.com

OTTAWA
▽▽▽ ▽▽▽ Fairmont Château Laurier ($$$)

A magnificent château-style hotel in the heart of the capital. It is famous for the fact that the original table linen and silverware went down with the *Titanic*. Sports facilities and restaurant.

✉ 1 Rideau Street ☎ 613/241-1414; 800/257-7544 (toll free); www.fairmont.com/laurier

▽▽▽▽ Lord Elgin Hotel ($$$)

A city landmark just across the street from the National Arts Centre. For what it offers it is remarkably good value. Restaurant.

✉ 100 Elgin Street ☎ 613/235-3333; 800/267-4298 (toll free); www.lordelginhotel.ca

SAULT STE. MARIE
▽▽▽▽ Algoma Water Tower Inn ($$)

Motor inn on the north side of town with excellent facilities. Some rooms have wood-burning stoves and pine furniture. Good place for children, with sports facilities and Lone Star Restaurant.

✉ 360 Great Northern Road ☎ 705/949-8111; 800/461-0800 (toll free); www.watertowerinn.com

THUNDER BAY
▽▽▽▽ White Fox Inn ($$–$$$)

In a large wooded estate, just south of the city with views of the hills. Well-furnished rooms and the best food in the area.

✉ 1345 Mountain Road ☎ 807/577-3699; 800/603-3699 (toll free); www.whitefoxinn.com

TORONTO
▽▽▽ ▽▽▽ Fairmont Royal York ($$$)

A Toronto landmark, this huge hotel (nearly 1,400 rooms) is connected to the train station and the underground PATH system. Amazing lobby with chandeliers and handpainted ceiling. Elegant rooms and a indoor skylit pool and fitness center.

✉ 100 Front Street West ☎ 416/368-2511; 800/257-7544 (toll free central reservations); www.fairmont.com/royalyork 🚇 Union

◆◆ ◆◆ **Windsor Arms ($$$)**

South of busy Bloor Street, close to Yorkville and the University of Toronto campus. Luxury five-story hotel with tastefully furnished rooms. The Courtyard Café (➤ 182–183) is excellent.

✉ 18 St. Thomas Street ☎ 416/971-9666; 877/999-2767 (toll free); www.windsorarmshotel.com ⓠ Bay

RESTAURANTS

KINGSTON

◆◆◆ **Chez Piggy ($$)**

A downtown restaurant with a garden patio. Popular with the local literati from Queens University and the Royal Military College.

✉ 68R Princess Street ☎ 613/549-7673; www.chezpiggy.com ⓒ Daily 11:30am–midnight (from 11am Sun)

◆◆◆ **The River Mill ($$–$$$)**

The quintessential Canadian dining room, overlooking the Cataraqui River. Quiet, relaxed, and conservative.

✉ 2 Cataraqui Street ☎ 613/549-5759; www.rivermill.ca ⓒ Mon–Fri 11:30–2:30, from 5 for dinner, Sat dinner only. Closed Sun

NIAGARA FALLS

◆◆◆ **Queenston Heights Restaurant ($$)**

Relaxed, affordable restaurant overlooking the Niagara River; outdoor patio in summer. Far from the bustle of the falls.

✉ 14184 Niagara Parkway ☎ 905/262-4274; www.niagaraparks.com/dining/queenstonres.php 🍴 Early May–Jan lunch, dinner and Sun brunch. Hours vary. Closed Feb–early May

NIAGARA-ON-THE-LAKE

◆◆ **Fan's Court ($$)**

On the attractive main street. Very good Chinese cuisine inside or outside in a pretty courtyard in summer.

✉ 135 Queen Street ☎ 905/468-4511 ⓒ Tue–Sun 12–9

OTTAWA
▽▽▽ Le Café ($$)
In the National Arts Centre overlooking the Rideau Canal. Pleasant outdoor terrace beside the canal in summer. Gourmet restaurant offering well-prepared Canadian specialties.

✉ 53 Elgin Street ☎ 613/594-5127; www.nac-cna.ca 🕐 Mon–Fri 12–11, Sat 5:30–11; winter: Mon–Fri 12–2, 5:30–11, Sat 5:30–11. Closed Sun

▽▽ Courtyard Restaurant ($$$)
Good Continental cuisine in an old stone building in a courtyard off Sussex Drive near the Byward Market (► 78).

✉ 21 George Street ☎ 613/241-1516; www.courtyardrestaurant.com
🕐 Mon–Sat 11:30–2, 5:30–9:30; Sun 11–2, 5–9

▽▽▽ Merlot ($$$)
Revolving restaurant atop the Marriott Hotel, with splendid views of the city and its site on the Ottawa River. Varied menu.

✉ 100 Kent Street ☎ 613/783-4212; www.merlotottawa.com 🕐 Mon–Sat 6pm–10pm, Sun 10:30–2, 6–10

SAULT STE. MARIE
▽▽▽ A Thymely Manner ($$)
In an old home. Uses only the best ingredients, herbs and spices for its menu of steak, pasta, and fish.

✉ 531 Albert Street East ☎ 705/759-3262; www.thymelymanner.com
🕐 Tue–Sat 5:30–11

TORONTO
▽▽▽ Bistro 990 ($$$)
French bistro that could be straight out of Paris. Serves excellent shrimp and filet mignon.

✉ 990 Bay Street ☎ 416/921-9990; www.bistro990.ca 🕐 Mon–Fri 12–10. Dinner only Sat and Sun 🚇 Wellesley

▽▽▽ ▽▽▽ Courtyard Café ($$$)
In the Windsor Arms Hotel near the University of Toronto campus. Luxurious restaurant with excellent rack of lamb and salmon, as

well as afternoon tea served in a relaxed atmosphere.

✉ 18 St. Thomas Street ☎ 416/971-9666; www.windorsarmshotel.com/cafe
🕐 Mon–Sat 7am–10 or 11pm, Sun brunch 10:30–2:30; closed Sun–Mon dinner 🚇 Bay

💎💎💎💎 Opus on Prince Arthur ($$$)

In a converted brownstone house close to Yorkville. Excellent Californian cuisine and an extensive wine list to choose from.

✉ 37 Prince Arthur Avenue ☎ 416/921-3105; www.opusrestaurant.com
🕐 Daily 5:30–11:30 🚇 St. George

💎💎 Pan on the Danforth ($$–$$$)

Upscale Greek dining with a rather eclectic menu. Good moussaka and a delicious casserole of chopped beef and potato.

✉ 516 Danforth Avenue ☎ 416/466-8158; www.panonthedanforth.com
🕐 Daily 12–11 (to midnight Fri–Sat) 🚇 Pape

💎💎💎💎 Scaramouche ($$$)

Just north of downtown. Romantic candlelit luxury, with splendid views of the Toronto skyline and acclaimed cuisine.

✉ 1 Benvenuto Place ☎ 416/961-8011; www.scaramoucherestaurant.com
🕐 Closed lunch and Sun 🚇 Summerhill

💎💎 Shopsy's Deli and Restaurant ($)

Shopsy's is a popular and noisy place close to the financial district with a huge menu of sandwiches, subs, soups and salads.

✉ 33 Yonge Street ☎ 416/365-3333; www.shopsys.ca 🕐 Mon–Wed 6:30am–11pm, Thu–Fri 6:30am–midnight, Sat 8am–midnight, Sun 8am–10pm 🚇 Union Station, King

SHOPPING

CENTERS AND MALLS
Canada One Factory Outlets

About 40 stores selling designer items with huge discounts, among them Liz Claiborne, Tommy Hilfiger and Ralph Lauren.

✉ 7500 Lundy's Lane, Niagara Falls ☎ 905/356-8989; 866/284-5781; www.canadaoneoutlets.com

Cataraqui Town Centre

Near the Trans-Canada Highway just west of the Cataraqui River. Has more than 140 stores, including The Bay, Zellers and Sears.

✉ 945 Gardiner Road, Kingston ☎ 613/389-7900;
www.cataraquitowncentre.ca

Toronto Eaton Centre

See page 79.

MARKETS
Byward Market

See page 78.

Kensington Market, Toronto

See pages 162–163.

St. Lawrence Market

Historic market building housing more than 120 vendors, including artisan food producers, fruit and vegetables, bakeries, delicatessens, wine and crafts.

✉ 92 Front Street East, Toronto ☎ 416/392-7120;
www.stlawrencemarket.com 🕐 Closed Sun–Mon 🚇 Union

CRAFTS AND OTHER SPECIALTIES
Algonquians Sweet Grass Gallery

Gallery owned by the Ojibwa. Exquisite sculptures in antler and soapstone, porcupine-quill jewelry and other traditional crafts.

✉ 668 Queen Street West, Toronto ☎ 416/703-1336 🚇 Osgoode then streetcar 501 west 🕐 Usually closed Sun

Dr. Flea's

Covered market north of the city with about 400 vendors selling all manner of objects. Farmers' market in summer.

✉ 8 Westmore Drive, Toronto ☎ 416/745-3532; www.drfleas.com
🕐 Sat–Sun only 🚇 Royal York then bus 73

Fireworks

See glass artists and work and then buy their beautiful creations, from wine glasses and vases to ornaments and marbles.

✉ 56 Queen Street, Kingston ☎ 613/547-9149; www.glassrootsstudio.com

Eskimo Art Gallery

Large collection of Inuit soapstone sculpture on display in a gallery reminiscent of the Arctic, with iceberg and tundra decorations.

✉ 12 Queens Quay West, Toronto ☎ 416/366-3000; 800/800-2008 (toll free); www.eskimoart.com 🚇 Union then Harbourfront streetcar 509 or 510

Joyce Seppala Designs

Inspired by Canada's northern landscapes, Joyce Seppala designs stunning clothes in fleece fabrics that are both practical and fun.

✉ 508 East Victoria Avenue, Thunder Bay ☎ 807/624-0022; www.joyceseppaladesigns.com 🕐 Closed Sun

ENTERTAINMENT

CHILDREN'S ENTERTAINMENT

Lorraine Kimsa Theatre for Young People

Established in 1966, this excellent theater stages thought-provoking plays, musicals and comedy for children of various ages.

✉ 165 Front Street East, Toronto ☎ 416/363-5131; 416/862-2222 (box office); www.iktyp.ca 🚇 Union Station, King then streetcar east

Valleyview Little Animal Farm

Farm animals of all types, train ride and puppet shows (weather permitting). Best to visit in spring, when there are lots of baby animals to see. Café.

✉ 4750 Fallowfield Road, Nepean, Ottawa ☎ 613/591-1126; www.vvlittleanimalfarm.com 🕐 Mar–Oct Tue–Sun (also holiday Mons)

THEATERS AND NIGHTCLUBS

Elgin and Winter Garden Theatres

Beautifully restored theaters (the Elgin is downstairs, the Winter Garden above it) producing drama, music and comedy year-round.

✉ 189 Yonge Street, Toronto ☎ 416/314-2901 🚇 Queen

Four Seasons Centre for the Performing Arts

Toronto's magnificent modern opera house, which opened in 2006, was custom designed to host opera and ballet and is home to the Canadian national opera and ballet companies.

✉ 145 Queen Street West, Toronto ☎ 416/363-6671 (admin); 416/363-8231 (box office); www.coc.ca 🚇 Osgoode

National Arts Centre

Performing arts center offering English and French theater, dance performances and classical and popular music shows year-round.

✉ 53 Elgin Street, Ottawa ✉ 613/947-7000; 866/850-2787 (toll free); www.nac-cna.ca

The Guvernment

Club complex on the waterfront offering big-name performers, local talent and DJs. Dress code for some shows.

✉ 132 Queens Quay East, Toronto ☎ 416/869-0045; www.theguvernment.com 🚇 Union then walk east

Second City

The famous comedy club that has nurtured such internationally renowned talent as Mike Myers and Dan Ayckroyd.

✉ 51 Mercer Street ☎ 416/343-0011; 800/263-4485; www.secondcity.com 🚇 Union Station

Shaw Festival Theatre

Theater primarily devoted to the production of the works of Irish writer George Bernard Shaw. The theater festival (Apr–Nov) also offers plays by other authors as well as comedy and musicals.

✉ 10 Queen's Parade, Niagara-on-the-Lake ☎ 905/468-2172; 800/511-7429 (toll free); www.shawfest.com

Stratford Festival of Canada

Canada's premier English-language theater company, producing the works of William Shakespeare and other classics (May–Nov).

✉ 55 Queen Street, Stratford ☎ 519/271-4040 (general enquiries); 800/567-1600 (box office); www.stratford-festival.on.ca

Sight Locator Index

This index relates to the maps on the covers. We have given map references to the main sights of interest in the book. Grid references in italics indicate sights featured on the town plans. Some sights within towns may not be plotted on the maps.

Index

Acknowledgements

The Automobile Association would like to thank the following photographers, companies and picture libraries for their assistance in the preparation of this book. Abbreviations for the picture credits are as follows: (t) top; (b) bottom; (c) centre; (l) left; (r) right; (AA) AA World Travel Library

4l Niagara Falls, AA/N Sumner; **4c** Jeanne Marche Square, Montreal, AA/J F Pin; **4r** Québec City, AA/N Sumner; **5l** Biosphère, Montreal, AA/J F Pin; **5r** Lake Memphremagog, AA/N Sumner; **6/7** Niagara Falls, AA/N Sumner; **8/9** Algonquin Provincial Park, AA/N Sumner; **10cl** Parc du Mont Tremblant, AA/N Sumner; **10br** Laurentides, AA/N Sumner; **10/11t** Cape Breton Island, AA/N Sumner; **10/11c** CBC Building Toronto, AA/J Davison; **11cr** Virginia Deer, Laurentides, AA/J F Pin; **11c** Montréal, AA/J F Pin; **11bl** Whale, Nova Scotia, AA; **12/13t** Lunenburg, AA/N Sumner; **12/13b** PEI lobster supper, AA/N Sumner; **13tr** Chocolates, AA/C Sawyer; **13cr** Montréal, AA/J F Pin; **14** Seafood platter, AA/J F Pin; **15t** Québec beer, AA/J F Pin; **15c** Maple syrup sign, AA/C Coe; **15b** Stratch Danial's Bar, Toronto, AA/J Beazley; **16** PEI lobster supper, AA/N Sumner; **16/17t** Canadian beer, AA/J F Pin; **16/17b** Chilliwack River, AA/P Timmermans; **18** Kensington Market, Toronto, AA/N Sumner; **18/19** Rogers Centre, AA/J F Pin; **19** Niagara Falls, AA/N Sumner; **20/21** Jeanne Marche Square, Montréal, AA/J F Pin; **22** Edwards Gardens, Toronto, AA/N Sumner; **24** Mounties, PEI, AA/N Sumner; **27** Lester Pearson International Airport, AA/J Beazley; **27** Montréal, AA/J F Pin; **28t** Amtrak Adirondack, AA/R Elliot; **28c** Canadian National Railways emblem, AA/J F Pin; **28b** Old Montréal, AA/J F Pin; **29** Toronto taxi, AA/N Sumner; **34/35** Québec City, AA/N Sumner; **36** Museum of Civilization, AA/J F Pin; **36/37** Museum of Civilization AA/J F Pin; **37** Museum of Civilization, AA/J F Pin; **38/39** Gulf of St Lawrence, AA/J F Pin; **40/1** Toronto's waterfront skyline, AA/J F Pin; **41** CN Tower, Toronto, AA/N Sumner; **42/43** Montréal, AA/J F Pin; **44/45t** Skylon Tower, Niagara Falls, AA/N Sumner; **44/45b** Niagara Falls, AA/N Sumner; **46/47t** Percé, AA/J F Pin; **46/47b** Gaspé Peninsula boat trip, AA/J F Pin; **48/49** Science North Building, AA/N Sumner; **49** Science North Building, AA/N Sumner; **50** Cannon, St John's AA/N Sumner; **50/51** Cabot Tower, St John's, AA/N Sumner; **52** Musee de-la-Fort, Quebec, AA/N Sumner; **52/53** Terrasse Dufferin, AA/N Sumner; **53** Québec, AA/N Sumner; **54/55t** Saguenay Fjord, AA/N Sumner; **54/55b** Beluga Whales, Saguenay Fjord, AA/N Sumner; **56/57** Biosphère, AA/J F Pin; **59** Chateau Lake Louise, AA/P Bennett; **61** Halifax, AA/N Sumner; **62** Steam Train, Ottawa, AA/J F Pin; **65** Rogers Centre, AA/J Davison; **66/67** Ontario Place, AA/N Sumner; **68** Royal Ontario Museum Toronto, AA/J Davison; **69** Fisheries Museum of the Atlantic, Lunenburg, AA/N Sumner; **71** Lighthouse, Prince Edward Island, AA/N Sumner; **73** Bay Street, Toronto, AA/N Sumner; **74/72** Gros Morne National Park, AA/N Sumner; **76/77** Glasses and napkins, Stockbyte; **78** Eaton Center, AA/J Beazley; **80/81** Lake Memphremagog, AA/N Sumner; **83** Gros Morne National Park, AA/N Sumner; **84/85** Halifax, AA/N Sumner; **86l** Citadel, Halifax, AA/N Sumner; **86r** Sentry, Halifax, AA/N Sumner; **86/87** Halifax, AA/N Sumner; **88** HMCS Sackville, Halifax, AA/N Sumner; **89** Annapolis Royal, AA/N Sumner; **90/91** Bonavista Peninsula, AA/J F Pin; **93** Queen Street, Fredericton, AA/N Sumner; **92/93** City Hall, Fredericton, AA/N Sumner; **94** Fundy National Park, AA/N Sumner; **94/95** Gros Morne National Park, AA/N Sumner; **96/97** Innu Community of Davis Inlet, Bryan & Cherry Alexander Photography/Alamy; **98/99** Fortress Louisbourg, AA/N Sumner; **99** Fisheries Museum of the Atlantic, Lunenburg, AA/N Sumner; **100l** Green Gables House, AA/N Sumner; **100r** PEI National Park, AA/N Sumner; **101** St. Andrews, AA/N Sumner; **102** St. John's, AA/N Sumner; **102/103** Eagle, Terra Nova National Park, AA/N Sumner; **103** Terra Nova National Park, AA/N Sumner; **104** Acadian rug hooking, AA/J F Pin; **111** Horse and trap, Montréal, AA/J F Pin; **112** Montréal, AA/J F Pin; **112/113** Basilique Notre-Dame, AA/J F Pin; **114/115** Le Biodôme, AA/J F Pin; **115** Chapelle de Notre-Dame-de-Bonsecours, AA/J F Pin; **116/117** Jardin Botanique de Montreal, AA/J F Pin; **117** Musee d'Archeologie, AA/J F Pin; **118** Musee d'Art Contemporain, AA/J F Pin; **118/119** Habitat '67, Montréal, AA/J F Pin; **120** Montréal Underground, AA/J F Pin; **121** Parc Olympique, AA/J F Pin; **122/123** Place d'Armes, Montréal, AA/J F Pin; **123** Montréal, AA/J F Pin; **124/125t** Québec City, AA/J F Pin; **124/125b** Notre-Dame Basilica, AA/N Sumner; **126/127** Chateau Frontenac, AA/N Sumner; **128/129** Holy Trinity Anglican Cathedral, AA/N Sumner; **130t** Place Royale, AA/J F Pin; **130b** Promenade des Gouverneurs, AA/N Sumner; **131** Baie-Saint-Paul, AA/N Sumner; **132** Montmorency Falls, AA/J F Pin; **132/133** St-Benoit-du-Lac, AA/N Sumner; **134** St-Jean Manoir Mauvide-Genest, AA/N Sumner; **134/135** Île de Orleans, AA/J F Pin; **135** Bedroom, Saine-Jean Manoir Mauvide-Genest, AA/N Sumner; **136/137** Saint-Sauveur, AA/N Sumner; **137t** Parc du Mont Tremblant, AA/N Sumner; **137b** Ville Mont Tremblant, AA/N Sumner; **138** St-Rose-du-Nord, AA/N Sumner; **138/139** Ste-Anne-de-Beaupré Cathedral, AA/J F Pin; **139** Ste-Anne-de-Beaupré Basilica, AA/N Sumner; **140t** Cap-de-la-Madeleine Shrine, Trois Rivieres, AA/N Sumner; **140b** Musée des Ursulines, Trois Rivieres, AA/N Sumner; **149** Toronto, AA/J Beazley; **150** Rideau Canal, AA/N Sumner; **150/151** Ottawa, AA/N Sumner; **152/153** Canada Museum, Courtesy of Canada Aviation Museum **154** National Gallery, Ottawa, AA/J F Pin; **155** National Gallery of Canada, AA/N Sumner; **156** Parliament Hill, AA/N Sumner; **156/157** Rideau Canal, Ottawa Locks, AA/J F Pin; **158/159** Toronto at night, AA/J F Pin; **159t** Toronto skyscrapers, AA/J Davison; **159b** Art Gallery of Ontario, AA/N Sumner; **160** Fountain, Art Gallery of Ontario, AA/J Davison; **160/161** Flags, Art Gallery of Ontario, AA/N Sumner; **162/163** Kensington Market, AA/N Sumner; **164l** Ontario Science Center, AA/J Davison; **164/165** Royal Ontario Museum, AA/J Beazley; **166** Hanlan's Point Beach, AA/N Sumner; **166/167** Hanlan's Point, AA/J Davison; **167t** Metro Zoo, AA/N Sumner; **167b** Yorkville, AA/J Davison; **168** Algonquin Provincial Park, AA/N Sumner; **169** Pentanguishene, AA/N Sumner; **170/171** Kingston, AA/N Sumner; **172** Niagara Falls, AA/N Sumner; **172/173** Fort Erie, AA/N Sumner; **173** Niagara Spanish Aero Cable Car, Niagara Parkway, AA/N Sumner; **174/175** Point Pelee National Park, AA/N Sumner; **176** Big Nickel, Sudbury, AA/N Sumner; **176/177** Thousand Island Parkway, AA/N Sumner; **178** Upper Canada Village, Stephen Saks Photography/Alamy.

Every effort has been made to trace the copyright holders, and we apologise in advance for any accidental errors. We would be happy to apply the corrections in the following edition of this publication.

Dear Reader

Your comments, opinions and recommendations are very important to us. Please help us to improve our travel guides by taking a few minutes to complete this simple questionnaire.

You do not need a stamp (unless posted outside the UK). If you do not want to cut this page from your guide, then photocopy it or write your answers on a plain sheet of paper.

Send to: **The Editor, AA World Travel Guides,**
FREEPOST SCE 4598, Basingstoke RG21 4GY.

Your recommendations...
We always encourage readers' recommendations for restaurants, nightlife or shopping – if your recommendation is used in the next edition of the guide, we will send you a **FREE AA Guide** of your choice from this series. Please state below the establishment name, location and your reasons for recommending it.

_____
_____
_____
_____
_____

Please send me **AA Guide** _____

About this guide...
Which title did you buy?
   AA _____
Where did you buy it?_____
When? m m / y y
Why did you choose this guide? _____
_____
_____
_____
_____

Did this guide meet your expectations?

Exceeded ☐   Met all ☐   Met most ☐   Fell below ☐

Were there any aspects of this guide that you particularly liked? _____
_____
_____
_____

continued on next page...

Is there anything we could have done better? _____

_____

_____

_____

About you...

Name (*Mr/Mrs/Ms*) _____

Address _____

_____

_____ Postcode _____

Daytime tel nos _____

Email _____

Please only give us your mobile phone number or email if you wish to hear from us about other products and services from the AA and partners by text or mms, or email.

Which age group are you in?
Under 25 ☐   25–34 ☐   35–44 ☐   45–54 ☐   55–64 ☐   65+ ☐

How many trips do you make a year?
Less than one ☐   One ☐   Two ☐   Three or more ☐

Are you an AA member? Yes ☐   No ☐

About your trip...

When did you book? m m / y y   When did you travel? m m / y y

How long did you stay? _____

Was it for business or leisure? _____

Did you buy any other travel guides for your trip? _____

If yes, which ones? _____

_____

_____

Thank you for taking the time to complete this questionnaire. Please send it to us as soon as possible, and remember, you do not need a stamp (*unless posted outside the UK*).

AA Travel Insurance call 0800 072 4168 or visit www.theAA.com